HERE *be* DRAGONS

An account of strange creatures
of Newfoundland and Labrador,
real or imaginary, we know not.

BRUCE HYNES

1 Stamp's Lane, St. John's, NL, Canada, A1E 3C9
WWW.BREAKWATERBOOKS.COM

LIBRARY AND ARCHIVES CANADA CATALOGUING IN PUBLICATION
Hynes, Bruce, 1940-
Here be dragons : strange creatures of Newfoundland and
Labrador / Bruce Hynes.
ISBN 978-1-55081-384-5

1. Animals--Newfoundland and Labrador--Folklore.
2. Animals, Mythical--Newfoundland and Labrador.
I. Title.
GR113.5.N5H96 2012   398.2'4509718   C2012-900921-0

We acknowledge the support of the Canada Council for the Arts, which last
year invested $154 million to bring the arts to Canadians throughout the
country. We acknowledge the Government of Canada through the Canada
Book Fund and the Government of Newfoundland and Labrador through the
Department of Tourism, Culture and Recreation for our publishing activities.

PRINTED AND BOUND IN CANADA.

Canada Council   Conseil des Arts   Canadä   Newfoundland
for the Arts   du Canada   Labrador

Breakwater Books is committed to choosing papers and materials for our
books that help to protect our environment. To this end, this book is printed
on a recycled paper that is certified by the Forest Stewardship Council®.

Dedicated to
all those
who said they
saw something
and
no one believed

CONTeNTS

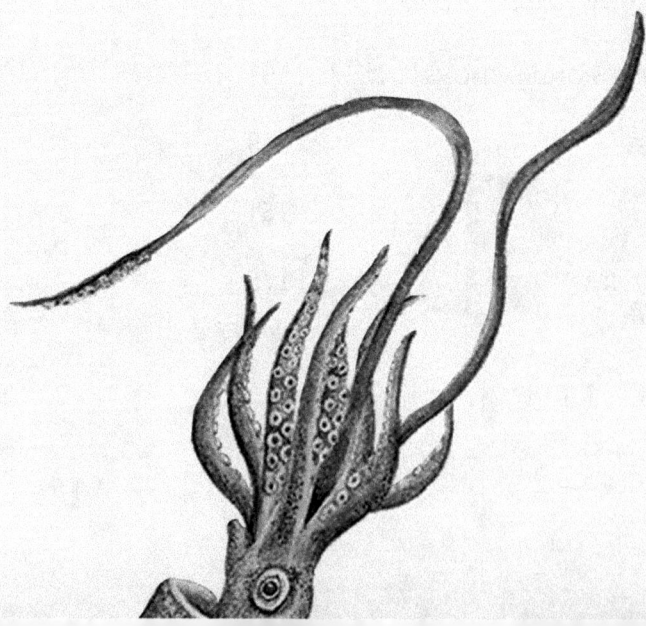

PREƒACE

THIS BOOK IS AN amalgamation of history, anecdotes, and folk tales. Inspired by a curious sighting in Terra Nova National Park and accounts from a few acquaintances, it is not intended to be a scientific work but for the reading enjoyment of those who are interested in the unexplained or unusual.

In the past hundreds of years, numerous blunders have been made regarding what is today called "cryptozoology," and many of these errors have been perpetuated. Scientists, as reluctant then as now to admit they did not know something, often fabricated explanations. However, many of these explained-away creatures refused to stay away and are as bewildering now as they were then.

In his book *The Lore of the Unicorn*, Odell Shepard observed that although few Europeans of the Middle Ages had ever seen a giraffe, lion, or elephant, they accepted the existence of these animals based upon evidence no better than that which attested to the existence of the unicorn. It is very difficult to say what others have or have not seen.

I vividly recall a strange creature that put in an appearance when I was a twelve-year-old. We had never seen our exotic visitor before, except in pictures. In the crush of siblings at the kitchen window and amid cries of "Luh! Luh! Luh!" and "Shhh!" we gazed in wonder at our first blue jay.

INTRODUCTiON

THE TERM CRYPTOZOOLOGY, FORMED from *crypto* (the Greek *kruptos* – hidden or concealed) and *zoology* (modern Latin, *zoologia* – the study of animals with reference to their structure, physiology, classification, and distribution) is fast becoming familiar to those who pay attention to what is going on around them. Coined by zoologist Bernard Heuvelmans, President of the International Society of Cryptozoology, it literally means the study of hidden animals. Used in reference to the search for creatures whose existence has been suggested but is so far unrecognized by a scientific consensus, it is, unfortunately, commonly thought to imply that their existence is highly unlikely. The discipline includes the search for living examples of animals thought to be extinct, such as dinosaurs or sabre-toothed tigers: animals whose existence lacks physical support but which appear in myths and legends, among them dragons, sea monsters, and wild animals dramatically outside their normal habitats, as with the famed big cats of the United Kingdom. Therefore, one of these hidden animals could be a stegosaur rediscovered in Africa, an altogether newlyfound animal of the Amazon, or a monkey chanced upon in Labrador.

Cryptozoology is seldom considered a credible scientific discipline in the strictest sense, particularly by pragmatists involved in other branches of study. Scientific journals rarely carry papers on the subject, formal education avoids mention of it, and only a few scientists are employed, even part-time, in the field. It is, nonetheless, a legitimate science; its accounts range from the sensationalism of an illusion or prank to the enlightening and interesting genuine observation.

Those involved in these studies are known as crypto-zoologists, and the beasts they study are often referred to as cryptids, a word proffered by John Wall in 1983. Noted cryptids include the sasquatch, the Loch Ness monster, and the chupacabra. While such creatures may have been reported by sincere witnesses and may be accepted as factual in areas where they are said to have been sighted, substantiation in the form of specimens or other hard evidence is still zealously sought. These apparent phantoms are not monsters except in that they are unknown to science. Though some few would probably argue this, cryptozoology does not deal with ghosts; demonic possession; paranormal, psychic, or supernatural phenomena; or, to my knowledge, unidentified flying objects (UFOs) or extraterrestrials.

So widespread is the fame of some cryptids (shaggy dog stories notwithstanding), many believe that somewhere, in dark and lonely places, they do exist. In 1990, Canada Post issued a series of stamps paying tribute to four of Canada's most persistent and best-known cryptids – the kraken, bigfoot or sasquatch, the *loup garou* (Quebec's version of the werewolf), and Ogopogo, British Columbia's famous lake monster.

At this point a brief cautionary tale is perhaps in order. The celebrated case of Great Britain's "Demon of Dartmoor" may serve to emphasize how easily we are sometimes misled.

The fearsome "Soe Orm."

In early summer 2007, uneasy residents of the Dartmoor area reported a strange and menacing beast roaming the moors. Indeed, they had even photographed the "hell hound," and the pictures appeared in national newspapers. In London, the *Daily Mail* of July 29 paid it particular attention, and speculation was rife; it was a wild boar, a bear, a panther, or some fiend from the darkest recesses of the netherworld.

The Centre for Fortean Zoology based in North Devon, the world's only full-time scientific organization for the study of anomalous beasts, was informed. Their zoological experts and investigators of reported cases of uncommon creatures said the news came as no surprise. Having been shown the pictures in early June, they had identified the beast as a large dog. That the photographs had made it into the national papers at all amazed them as they knew from the start it was not worth pursuing.

ON AUGUST 3 THE *Daily Mail* printed an explanation, though it was not accepted by everyone. Lucinda Reid, a cook at a school in Heathfield near Newton Abbot, Devon, read of the devilish phantom and came forward to say that she knew the identity of the monster: It was her two-year-old 76-kilogram Newfoundland dog, Troy. The good-natured and curious Troy enjoyed exploring his surroundings and spent much time wandering the area. Ms. Reid thought the whole affair hilarious. Despite this blow, monster hunters have no doubt that outlandish creatures really do roam Dartmoor.[1] This tale is included here because it is peculiar and features one of Newfoundland's least likely monsters.

An unlikely monster.

There is no reason, of course, why Newfoundland and Labrador should not be home to undiscovered wildlife. After all, scientists recently examined 565-million-year-old rock at Mistaken Point and discovered what they think is the earliest evidence of animal locomotion on the planet. The fossilized tracks found here on the pre-Cambrian sea floor were made by *Ediacarans,* the earliest of complex organisms. Debate continues over what they looked like and even what they were.[2]

Some of their descendants may still be around. Back in 1938, the coelacanth, a deep-sea creature supposed by experts to have been extinct for more than 65 million years, was discovered to be alive and well. Brought to shore by a fishing trawler at East London, South Africa, it was seen by Marjorie Courtenay-Latimer, curator of a small museum. While visiting the trawler's captain, who often let her check his catch for unfamiliar specimens, she spotted an oddly shaped blue-grey fin protruding from the pile of fish. Taking her find back to the museum, she compared it with images of known species and soon realized it was no ordinary fish. The world was fascinated, and a major debate began about how the bizarre lobe-finned beast fit into the evolution of land animals. Some of the mysterious specimens you will meet in the ensuing pages may also be living fossils.

1. Rebecca Camber, *Daily Mail* (London), July 29, 2007, & Jean Tiley, *Guardian News* (London), August 4, 2007.
2. Alexander G. Liu, Duncan McIlroy & Martin D. Brasier, "First Evidence for Locomotion in the *Ediacara Biota* from the 565 Ma. Mistaken Point Formation, Newfoundland," *Geology* 38, no. 2 (February 2010), 123–36.

chapter

one

THE KRA*k*EN'S SPAWN

STRANGE CREATURES OF ASSORTED shapes and sizes have always inhabited the imaginary universe of humans, ranging from the profound to the ridiculous. Throughout history, we have populated the waters of our planet with monstrosities that gobble up mariners like popcorn. Tales of sea monsters are found in virtually all cultures that have contact with the oceans, and eyewitness accounts come from around the world.

The province of Newfoundland and Labrador consists of a sea-girt island and an immense, largely unpopulated, northern region also with an extensive coastline, so we will begin with anomalies of the sea. These form the greatest portion of our mysterious animals; some of them are thought to be among the more primitive of the world's inhabitants. In truth, many may well be holdovers of earlier times, much like the coelacanth, the horseshoe crab, and various crocodilia.

PERHAPS THE GIANT SQUID should not be mentioned here at all – it has been proven to exist beyond a doubt and seldom

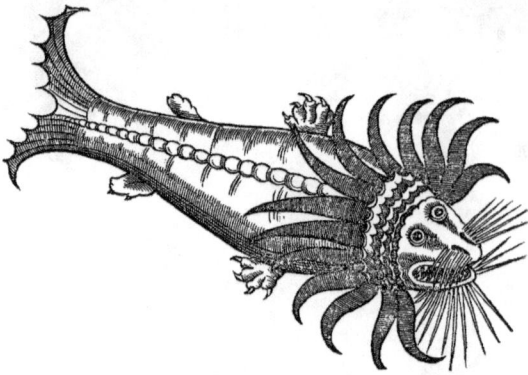

springs to mind when sea monsters are mentioned. Still, there are those who would disagree with that way of thinking, because as far as we know, the first giant squid appeared in historic times as the legendary kraken of Norse mythology. This horror was first reported in the waters off Norway and said to be a couple of kilometres in circumference; time and familiarity have reduced it to a mere shadow of its former self.

Danish bishop, historian, antiquary, and author Erik Pontoppidan described the kraken in 1752 and noted that the surrounding water had been darkened by its protective mechanism. This well-nigh confirms that the tales were inspired by the giant squid, which counts among its defences this familiar ink or sepia.[1]

The kraken survived more as legend than animal for many years in the folklore of early Newfoundland and Labrador. Tales of a giant creature with arms and tentacles that could embrace a ship – crushing its hull – terrified generations of mariners. In some cases vessels were said to have been sucked down in the tremendous vortex left by a submerging kraken. Many men of science thought the rare ambergris produced by sperm whales and sometimes found on beaches was the kraken's excrement.

Often confused with octopuses, which attack humans only when threatened, the giant squid is an efficient predator. The name "devilfish" has been used worldwide for a variety of odd or nasty sea creatures, but in Newfoundland it invariably refers to the giant squid. It is perhaps the basis of many sea monster tales, since we know the beast can easily weigh 500 kilograms and in its entirety can exceed 20 metres in length. *Architeuthis* are the most highly developed of invertebrates: Their eyes are almost exact duplicates of human eyes except for being more acute and often bigger than basketballs. They have the largest eyes of any living animal – the ocular diameter may exceed 40 centimetres. Compare this with the usual 24-centimetre basketball.

CAPTAIN GEORGE CARTWRIGHT, FAMED trader and explorer of Newfoundland and Labrador, told of how impressed fishermen had been when they found a huge deceased specimen floating on the Grand Banks on May 27, 1785.

A decade later, convoy escort HMS *Boston* voyaged to Newfoundland and among her crew was Aaron Thomas of Hertfordshire, a mere able seaman but one whose literacy and intelligence secured for him the position of captain's steward. Today he is remembered mostly for his comprehensive journal.

Thomas was quite skeptical of the existence of the common squid, much less a giant version of this strange creature, but his disbelief diminished after he had seen the lesser variety. He told of it in his writings of 1794:

> There is a Fish found on the Banks and on the Shores of Newfoundland after the Capelin time is over which is the most curious I ever saw from its shape and colour and propertys. Its weight and length is about equal to a small Herring, its composition is a transparent jelly with a small substance in the middle...Its formation is very singular. Its Tail is like the Fluke of an anchor; from the head part extends Six [actually, there are ten] fibrous and glutinous tubes ending in a point, the inner part looking like a saw has the property of adhering to any pungent substance it toucheth. Within its mouth is a Beak alike and as hard as

Captain Cartwright.

the Beak of a Parrot. Right down the centre of his gummy body is a tube, a part of which is filled with a Liquid, as Black as Ink. This engine, so charged, he can command as freely as an Elephant can his Trunk, and whenever a Squid is hauled out of the Sea he is sure to discharge this Liquid at you, he generally aims at your face...

However he remained somewhat doubtful of the existence of a giant of the species:

He is also said to be the largest Fish in the Sea, but this is fabulous. I never met a person who ever saw one that weighed more than Four Pounds [1.8 kilograms], but I have heard storys at St. John's of one being caught on the Grand Banks which Eight men could not haul into the Boat, and also of the horn [as the two longer tentacles were often called] of one being found cast ashore in Freshwater Bay which Two men with difficulty could carry.[2]

While Thomas obviously did not believe a creature of such exaggerated proportions existed, his statement established that others had seen them around Newfoundland, at least occasionally.

OTHER STORIES EMERGE FROM dusty records. A man engaged in the Labrador fishery in the mid-1800s related how he and two mates had escaped such a brute. Their small schooner of around 30 tonnes was in the relatively calm waters of an inlet when, inexplicably and without warning, it began to sink. Water was rapidly approaching the gunwales, yet the boat's well was dry. They were baffled and straightaway put the ship's boat over the side. The trio were nonplussed when this action disturbed a huge squid clutching the bottom of their vessel, seemingly intent on pulling it down. The monstrosity released the schooner, and all seven-plus metres of it submerged and shot away.

According to the United States *Annual Report of the Commissioner of Fish and Fisheries* for 1879, two squid, one of 12 metres and the other 14, washed up on the beach at Lamaline in the winter of 1870. In the same report, amateur naturalist Reverend Doctor Moses Harvey referred to a statement made to him by a Reverend M. Gabriel regarding two specimens measuring respectively 12 and nearly 14 metres in length, which were likewise cast upon the beach at Lamaline in the winter of 1870–1871. In all probability, Harvey meant A. E. Gabriel, rector of Lamaline's Church of St. Mary the Virgin from 1860–1874. Rather than two incidents, as implied by the *Annual Report*, it is without doubt a case of one corroborating the other.

Another specimen was found floating on the surface of the Grand Banks in October 1871 by the schooner *B.D. Haskins*, Captain Campbell of Gloucester, Massachusetts. It was put to good use by blasé dorymen who chopped it up for bait.[3] A reddish squid was driven into shallow water at Coomb's Cove in late autumn of 1872. Its body alone was three metres long and one arm, a little larger than a man's wrist in diameter, was almost 13 metres, giving it an overall length of nearly 16 metres. It was said to have weighed in excess of a tonne,[4] though this was perhaps an exaggeration.

Newfoundland's first supposedly "substantiated" encounter with a giant squid is said to have taken place in 1873 when one attacked a minister and a young boy who were in a dory just off Bell Island. While nearly everyone who has written of these incidents has mentioned this occurrence, no confirmation or further details have been found.

Bishop's Rock, in Conception Bay, was a favourite fishing ground, and men arose early to get there first, especially if they were alone due to a mate being ill or otherwise absent. The first to arrive took the best station, and later arrivals would leave him to it and move to other areas farther off shore. However, by 1873

The kraken or poulpe colossal.

the rock was considered somewhat sinister by those who frequented the grounds. One day, a man who was fishing there alone vanished from his boat and was never seen again. The boat was anchored safely enough, but there was no indication of what had become of him. Soon after another man disappeared; his boat was found floating a short distance from the rock. Neither case gave any indication of what had become of the missing men. Nothing in their boats had been disturbed; a fish-line was found still hanging over the side of one, but that was all. Afterward, fishermen began to avoid the rock, especially if working alone.

According to Frank Aubrey's "A Newfoundland Terror," in October of that year Sam Wilney and his mate Pat Daly, both of St. John's, set out for the rock.[5] It was a calm day, and while Wilney rowed, Daly set about preparing some lines and nets; then Wilney's stretcher (a strip of wood set athwart the bottom of the boat for a rower to brace his feet against) broke. Intending to repair the stretcher, Wilney asked Daly to find their axe in the locker under a pile of rope. They were in no particular hurry as they were drifting in the right direction all the while.

As Wilney completed his stretcher and put the axe down, Daly, who had been looking across at the rock, said in a low voice that he had seen, if he believed in such taradiddle, a "great long t'ing rise out of th' water, wigglin' and twistin' about like a sarpent." Wilney, in good humour, voiced his disbelief in crude terms, but Daly insisted. Finally, they decided to investigate and rowed over to where Daly had seen the mysterious object. Wilney stopped pulling when they were about 15 metres from the rock, and as the boat drifted around broadside to it, they could see what appeared to be a great dark mass of seaweed in the calm water.

Wilney snorted derisively that it was nothing but seaweed; they were totally unprepared and completely horrified when something lashed out from the kelp and threw itself across their small craft. Daly described it as being like a long serpent lying across the boat. Rocking violently, the boat was being dragged inexorably toward the rock when a second rubbery arm was flung over it. Evidently, the creature had been lying in wait holding on to the rock with a couple of its arms. Daly said he could see more than seven metres of the tentacles grasping the boat.

With water spilling in over the gunwale, the boat was in imminent danger of being upset; Wilney sat petrified until Daly cried out for him to chop the tentacles off. Grabbing the axe, Wilney cut through both arms, the pieces falling, writhing, into the boat which at once righted itself. Seizing the oars, he brought the boat's head around in an attempt to row away, when up out of the water arose an evil apparition – four or five great arms and a thing as "big as a tub wit' eyes as big as soup-plates." They knew then what it was: a tremendous devilfish.

Now discouraged, their assailant released its grip and plunged beneath the surface, leaving the water around the wildly lurching boat black with ink. The creature's arms were more than five metres long and nearly a metre in circumference at the thickest part. There is no proof to substantiate this tale, but it is certainly an interesting one; other incidents in the same area also lend it credence.

Alexander Murray, Chief of the Newfoundland Geological Survey (said by some to seldom reduce the importance of his experiences), claimed to have measured the arms as well and had the pieces taken away and preserved in spirits at the museum. It was calculated that the full length of the arms they had chopped off would have been more than nine metres.

The story got around, and from that time on Bishop's Rock was known to local fishermen as Sea Devil's Rock and was avoided. Wilney claimed that he could never look at it, even from a distance, without feeling ill. He also said that some three weeks later a great storm threw another of the behemoths on shore a few kilometres away. Though of a similar size, it was not the same creature as it had its full complement of arms.

Frank Aubrey cites Reverend Gabriel's report that a giant of more than 14 metres in length had washed ashore near Lamaline and that another of nearly 25 metres had been found in the same general area, but gives the date as October 1873. Apparently these statements were also confirmed by Reverend Harvey.[6] Likely, this was the same pair Gabriel reported in the winter of 1870–1871. If this was the case, however, the last mentioned had grown by nine metres.

Later that same October, on the 26th, the first irrefutable proof, at least in modern times, of the animal's existence came to light. Daniel Squires, Theophilus Picco, and the latter's 12-year-old son Tom, who was at their skiff's tiller, were fishing for herring off Portugal Cove. Seeing a strange object off toward Bell Island that they took to be wreckage floating on the surface, they rowed over for a closer look – and a closer look they got.

One of them poked the unrecognizable hulk with a boat-hook, and it became a demon from the pit. With what they believed to be rage in its coldly staring green eyes, it flung a limber arm around the boat while its frightful beak chewed into

the gunwale. Water poured in as another arm encircled the skiff threatening to pull it under, or at least upset it. It certainly would have done so, but quick-witted Tom grabbed a hatchet and cut off a few sections of the powerful cablelike tentacles; the disheartened squid departed amid a spray of inky fluid.

Safely back on shore but still shaking, Picco swore the squid's tail had been about two metres wide. Tom did not think the event at all remarkable and threw the shorter tentacle to the dogs, but the long slender one, with suckers only at its tip, he kept; he thought he might make it into a painter for his boat!

Fishermen's tales of monstrous squid with arms from seven to ten metres in length had long since triggered the interest of Reverend Harvey. So it was that when fishermen of Portugal Cove recommended that Tom take his remnants to Harvey, the youngster showed up at that worthy's door inquiring if he wanted to buy the "'arn off a big squid?"

Harvey met with the still distracted fishermen, who asserted the creature was not less than 22 metres long; he confirmed this estimate by drawing a comparison between its tentacles and the corresponding bits of the common squid. He calculated its weight to be about 550 kilograms.[7]

It was the world's first significant proof of the fabulous devilfish, and the Reverend was ever afterward known by the misnomer of "Octopus" Harvey. England's Natural History Society published an article written by Harvey, and the giant squid was named *Architeuthis harveyi* in his honour. fortunately, this designation lasted but a short time, as it did not meet the specifications of the Code of Zoological Nomenclature. The correct name is now *Architeuthis dux*. The event was put out of mind for years, but Harvey's photograph of Tom's tentacle remained on view at the museum in St. John's until recently.

In 1861, the French gunboat Alecton *attempted to capture a giant squid, and though only a portion of the animal was secured, it led to wider recognition of the genus.*

It was a banner year for large squid. Soon after, on November 25, another was snagged in a herring net at Logy Bay. The unexpectedly large catch put up a terrific struggle; when the delighted fishermen finally got the net to the surface, they were appalled to find a sea monster enmeshed in it rather than the anticipated bumper load of herring. Enormous eyes glared at them and supple tentacles struck out and latched onto their boat. A half-hour battle ended when a fisherman's knife hit home at the back of the creature's head, near the "funnel," practically decapitating it. Dragging their prize to shore, they contacted Harvey who set out at once to take possession of the remains of the ten-metre-long creature. At Logy Bay the fisherman who had killed it spoke to Harvey and declared emphatically that he would not tackle another of the breed for all the money in the world.[8]

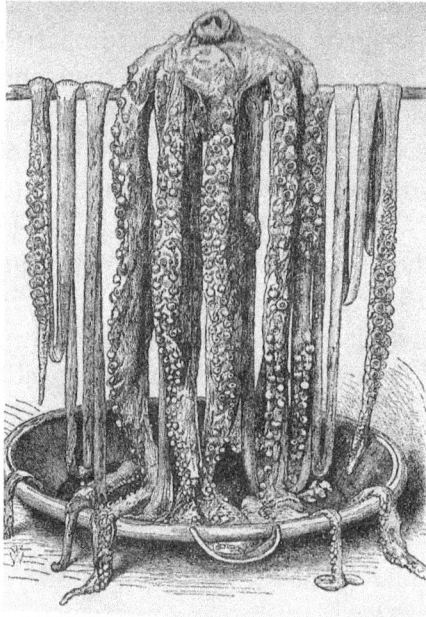

Harvey's big squid hanging from his sponge bath

The next year, the 136-tonne schooner *Peril*, Captain James Flood, was attacked by a sea monster off the south coast. Flood's report, written up in *News World* of July 1874, claimed that he had, against the advice of crewman and Newfoundlander Bill Darling, taken a shot at the creature with a rifle before the assault began. Infuriated, the 11-metre-long animal flung itself at the schooner, and wrapping enormous tentacles and arms around the masts, dragged most of itself on board. Finally, it wedged its barrel-like body between the mainmast and the aft hatch; the crew, under Darling's direction, hacked at it with axes and knives in an attempt to free the ship. When the monster (still clutching the masts) slipped back over the side, its sheer weight dragged the *Peril* onto her beam ends, and she filled with water and sank.

Those on-board *Peril* were rescued by the American schooner *Strathowen*, whose captain and crew had witnessed the bizarre battle. The story was told throughout the United States by numerous newspapers in 1874, with most accounts warning the world's seafarers to keep an eye out for such hazards.[9]

It should be pointed out that a news report in *The Times* of London stated that on July 4, 1874, the *Strathowen*, a steamer, was bound from Mauritius to Rangoon, a long way from our south coast, and that the schooner was the *Pearl* under a Captain Floyd. Bernard Heuvelmans questioned the veracity of the account, and the *Strathowen* is not to be found in Lloyd's *Register* or at any other institute here or in Britain. The similarity of the names of the vessels and captains raises some flags as well.[10] Also, it is perhaps significant that the incident – if it took place at all – occurred shortly after the 1869 publication of *Twenty Thousand Leagues Under the Sea*.

At Grand Bank, in December 1874, an eight-metre-long specimen washed ashore and, again, its tail was fed to the dogs. Later that year, or perhaps early in 1875, another was found at

Harbour Grace, but it, too, was destroyed before it could be examined. In October of the following year, another was chopped up for bait by Grand Bank fishermen, and on November 20, 1876, a partial specimen was found at Hammer Cove, Green Bay, having been mostly eaten by foxes and seagulls. Difficulty in finding a complete squid was frustrating, but finally one showed up.

Residents of Catalina were impressed by the immense squid that washed ashore there on September 24, 1877. About 12 metres long, it was still alive when found and yielded a near-perfect specimen. Its arrival and demise were written up in *The Canadian Illustrated News*:

> The tail had got fast on a rock. In its desperate efforts to escape, the ten arms darted about in all directions, lashing the water into foam, the thirty-foot [9 metres] tentacles in particular making lively play as it shot them out and endeavoured to get a purchase with their powerful suckers, so as to drag itself into deep water. It was only when it became exhausted and the tide receded that the fishermen ventured to approach it. It died soon after the ebb tide which left it high and dry on the beach.[11]

When the squid was exhibited in St. John's, the length of its tentacles was confirmed to be more than nine metres long and its girth between two and three metres. Its body was nearly three metres long, its head more than a metre, and the tail a full metre.[12]

Yet another was found on a Trinity Bay beach in October but was washed away before it could be examined. However, on November 21, John Duffet of Lance Cove found one still alive,

Jules Verne's enormously popular 1869 book, Vingt mille lieues sous les mers *(that is,* Twenty Thousand Leagues Under the Sea*), may have inspired some reports of monsters.*

The Catalina squid.

having been borne ashore by a spring tide and an onshore
wind. He asserted that the stream of fluid it ejected ploughed a
furrow in the sand about nine or ten metres long and of
considerable depth. It died when the tide went out and Duffet,
measuring it carefully, found that its body was more than three
metres long and its tentacular arms, ten metres. Residents cut
the body open for no particular reason and left it on the beach.
Being a frugal and industrious man, Duffet cut it up and put
much of it on his garden; the remainder was carried off by the
tide. In conversation with Harvey, he mentioned that another
big squid had come ashore about eight kilometres up the bay the
previous month, and it too had been cut up by fishermen and
used to fertilize their gardens.[13] In this out-of-the-way place no
one dreamt that it might be worth anything.

Thimble Tickle, a passage between several islands south of Leading Tickles and a few kilometres north of Glovers Harbour, was the setting for a more spectacular appearance. On November 2, 1878, Joseph Martin, Stephen Sperring, and another fisherman were not far from shore when they saw a sizeable object they thought to be wreckage from some shipping disaster. Curious, they rowed up to it and to their amazement found it to be an enormous and grotesque marine creature with large glassy eyes, frantically thrashing about its arms, tentacles, and tail. It had been grounded on a shoal by the ebbing tide, so they took advantage of the creature's situation and hooked it with a grapnel, then hauled a line ashore and tied it firmly to a tree. It struggled for quite some time, but died as the water continued to recede. Heedless of its possible value to science or the opportunity to say "I told you so" to skeptics, they too chopped up their catch to feed their dogs. Its total length was 16.8 metres, of which the body accounted for 6.1 metres and its tentacles 10.7 metres.[14] Estimated to weigh 2.2 tonnes – again, perhaps a gross overestimate – it was certainly a big one.

In 1988, famed author and scientist Arthur C. Clarke produced the video series *Mysterious World*. On the show, Memorial University's Frederick Aldrich, an international authority on giant squid, examined a six-metre-long immature specimen and offhandedly commented, "I believe the giant squid reach an approximate maximum size of something like 150 feet [45.72 metres]." Why he said this is hard to fathom as it would appear, from all available evidence, that the largest then known was the 16.8 metre specimen from Thimble Tickle.[15]

Though, it has been said that other specimens from around the island have overshadowed the Thimble Tickle squid by wide margins, there has certainly been no confirmation of this. Indeed, Thimble Tickle's whopper earned itself a spot in the *Guinness Book of Records* as the largest squid in the world; in fact, the largest invertebrate.

Fisherman Joseph Martin, c. 1880.

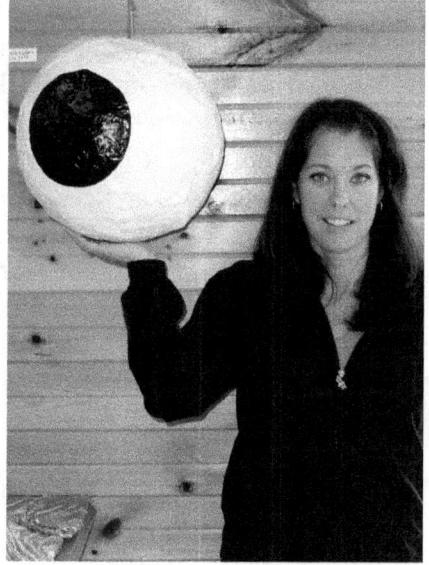

Lori-Lynn Collins, great-great-granddaughter of Martin, and a replica of the big squid's eyeball.

Replica of the Thimble Tickle monster at the site of its landing.

This conservative publication also agreed with the estimated weight of a stunning two tonnes. To mark the occasion of its recognition as such and to serve as a tourist attraction, a life-sized model of the squid was commissioned and built near the beach at Glovers Harbour in 2001, not far from the site of its death.

Harvey gave an account of another specimen in a letter to *The Boston Traveller*. Found dead on the shore after a heavy gale, on December 2, 1878, by fisherman William Budgell of Three Arms, it had been cut up for the dogs. Harvey said his informant was a very intelligent man who was in the area on business and had arrived at Budgell's house shortly after the latter had arrived home with the remains. The body was 4.5 metres from the tip of its beak to the end of its tail, it was more than 3.5 metres in circumference at the thickest part of the body, and one of its short arms was nearly five metres long.[16]

Only a pair of arms were found near Brigus in October 1878, but the disappointment was alleviated somewhat when, around the beginning of November, the small inlet of James Cove, Bonavista Bay, hosted another large squid. Thomas Moores and several others saw something moving about in the water not far from their stage. Getting into a punt, they rowed out to it and stared aghast at immense eyes, disconcertingly staring back at them. One of the men poked it tentatively with an oar and the beast immediately struck out for shore where it ran aground. After it had shuffled off this mortal coil, the men succeeded in getting a rope around it, hauling it up on the beach. It was 11.6 metres in total length, with the body being about 2.7 metres. Its tentacles were nearly nine metres long.[17] *The Morning Chronicle* (St. John's) of December 9 reported that it had been driven ashore, died, and was then cut up for bait and dog food.[18] In those days had the Devil himself been hove up on a beach, he would have been cut up for bait.

Alexander Murray, who recorded Wilney's and Daly's 1873 encounter with a squid, came to the attention of the public again when he repeated an account he had directly from a man named Pike, who had found a squid washed up near St. John's in November 1873. This specimen was entered into the official *Architeuthis* list as having a head-and-body length of 2.35 metres, which leads us to suspect that Murray was, at times, truthful. Later, he told of another he had heard of from a Mr. Haddon who reported his squid as more than 27 metres long.

Murray caused some excitement among squid fans who believe he cast doubt on all his previous accounts when he told of a specimen that measured 80 feet (24 metres) from *beak* to *tail*![19] Surely, anyone who had paused a moment to put their mental machinery in gear would have realized that this was a typesetter's error and it had really been eight feet (2.4 metres).

In April 1880, portions of a squid were found floating about on the Grand Banks by the Gloucester fishing schooner *William H. Oakes*, Captain O. A. Whitten, but by now the fishing public had ceased to be stunned by such minor finds.

However, an 8.5-metre-long dead squid was found floating along the shore at Portugal Cove on November 10, 1881. Though in poor condition, it was purchased by a Mr. Morris, who after he had it recorded by Water Street photographer E. Lyons, put it on ice and shipped it off via SS *Catima* to E. M. Worth of New York, for exhibition at his 14th Street Dime Museum in the Bowery.

Worth's museum was among the most popular in America during the late 1800s, and by year's end the Newfoundland devilfish had been added to its displays. To promote the attraction, posters were distributed throughout New York; *The Evening Mercury* of St. John's brought this fact to everyone's attention on January 5, 1882, when it exulted:

A huge woodcut at the head of the advertising placard showed ten arms flung out, two of them grasping and curling round two human beings who are writhing in agony.

Competition among St. John's newspapers of the era was keen, and animosity often spilled over into news items. This one carried a barb aimed at *The Evening Telegram*'s editor:

Some people here who have examined this woodcut, say that one of the sufferers grappled by the Devil Fish has a striking resemblance to the head editor of The Evening Telegram, his photograph having been forwarded along with the fish; but we are unable to concur in this opinion. The figure in the woodcut is not nearly handsome enough.

Having generated some amusement at the expense of his rival, the editor continued:

Our native in the museum is in excellent company. Near it reposes The Virginian Double Baby; The Embalmed Egyptian Baby, 3,000 years old; A Happy Family of Mischievous Monkeys; and a Den of Living Serpents complete the attractions.[20]

By now sightings of giant squid were being accepted with some equanimity, as illustrated by this terse news item from Twillingate in 1891:

Fought with Octopus – Fought a Devil Fish Under Water: On Saturday morning the divers, Messrs. Llewellyn and McHardy, who are engaged in repairing the water pipes in the Narrows, had a narrow and exciting experience of a fight with an octopus, commonly known as a devil fish.[21]

No doubt they had become involved with a squid, but in Twillingate at least, it does not seem to have aroused a great deal of concern, journalistic or otherwise.

However, there was still some excitement in store for others. On a bright August morning in 1912, Josiah Sheppard of Lark Harbour followed his daily routine and set out in his dory for the nearby fishing grounds. Because of contrary winds, his brother Henry towed him out to the area with his motor boat where he set to work. After some hours off Wee Bauld, Josiah had only a half-quintal of fish, so he and Henry decided to try their luck elsewhere. Josiah joined his brother in the motor boat; when they reached the new location, he returned to his dory and let it drift off about 200 metres astern.

Josiah was about to put his hand-lines out when an immense creature broke the surface beside him. The monster lifted its head over the gunwale; Josiah declared that it first stared at him, then at the fish in the bottom of the dory. The petrified man gaped as great tentacles seized the boat and pulled it under, leaving him thrashing about in the water. He cried out to Henry, but just then his dory popped to the surface and he clambered in. Here he remained, huddled in the bottom, until his brother arrived and hauled him into the motorboat.

Sheppard described the devilfish as having a fearsome mouth of more than a metre across and marks of the behemoth's bite, about 75 centimetres long, were quite evident in the dory's gunwale. The monster had a white belly and black back, and was obviously some sort of squid or cuttlefish. Sheppard was certain that only the presence of fish in the dory saved his life; had they not been there he would have become the mollusc's lunch instead.[22]

If you think the possibility of such an encounter is far-fetched, consider the following: the Humboldt squid, relatively small when compared to the giant squid, can grow to 2.5 metres long and weigh up to 45 kilograms. Recently, two Mexican fishermen were dragged from their boats by a school of these and mangled so badly they were unidentifiable. Warnings of the northern migration of these creatures were issued along the Pacific Coast notifying those tempted to play in the water of the danger.

A particularly foolhardy giant squid made at least three assaults on the Royal Norwegian Navy's 15,000-tonne auxiliary tanker *Brunswick* in the 1930s. The onslaught was deliberate; each time, the squid pulled alongside the ship, paced it, then suddenly veered and threw its tentacles about the hull. The intractable beast was unable to get a good grip on the steel surface – having tried the tactic once too often, it slid off and was killed by the propellers.[23]

One of these giant squid was found on the beach at Dildo, Trinity Bay, on December 19, 1933, by Richard Gosse and Reuben Reid. It was more than nine metres long and weighed in at a respectable 260 kilograms. As was done in Thimble Tickle, a replica was constructed to mark the event and is still on display at the Dildo Area Interpretation Centre's museum.[24]

Another washed ashore at Holyrood on November 12, 1935, and was captured by Harbour Main fisherman Joe Ezekiel. He sold the specimen to a scientist for ten dollars, who then stored it in the local Fisheries Department freezer. Unfortunately for the investor, the freezer caught fire a few days later and his prize was incinerated.

A truly notable and well-documented incident took place on Tuesday, March 25, 1941. While crossing the Atlantic, the 10,000-tonne HMS *Cilicia* received an urgent radio message from *Britannia*, 8,000 tonnes, which was some distance away, to the effect that she was being attacked by a German surface raider. *Cilicia* received no further messages, and assuming that the enemy had been successful in their efforts, continued about her business.

However, at 6:25 a.m. on Friday, *Cilicia* sent a boarding party to check out the SS *Bachi*, a small Spanish tramp. They found the Spaniard had arrived on the scene of *Britannia*'s destruction in time to pick up 63 of the 312 who had been on board. A dozen survivors told how, as they clung to their lifeboat, the arms of a giant squid encircled one of their number and pulled him beneath the surface. Since he did not reappear, his comrades took it for granted that he had been eaten.[25] A tentacle clutched the arm of Lieutenant R. E. Grinan-Cox, Indian Army, who, though released by the creature, carried the scar of its grip to his grave.

During World War II, large numbers of fishing trawlers, having been converted into minesweepers, were placed in service by the combatant nations. The trawlers were ideally suited to the task, and their crews proved remarkably adaptable to minesweeping techniques. It is said that on one such vessel, lying off the Maldive Islands in the Indian Ocean, a member of the crew, one A. G. Starkey, was on deck fishing. Suddenly, something appeared alongside in the water. He wrote:

> As I gazed, fascinated, a circle of green light glowed in my area of illumination. This green unwinking orb I suddenly realized was an eye. The surface of the water undulated with some strange disturbance. Gradually I realized that I was gazing at almost point-blank range at a huge squid.[26]

Starkey went on to say that he had walked the length of the vessel and found the monster's tail at one end of it and the clubs, the tips of its tentacles, at the other. Perhaps Mr. Starkey was sparing with the truth, but if not, *his* squid was 53 metres long! This tale has turned up in many publications, and often Starkey's initials and the length of his vessel change. Such variations tend to cast doubt on the entire story for which, in any event, no concrete evidence or plausible sources can be found.

In the 1960s, there was a sudden embarrassment of big squid around Newfoundland. In December 1961, a relatively small representative of the species came ashore at King's Cove, Bonavista Bay. On October 23, 1964, one was found floating

A trawler typical of that on which Starkey sailed.

near Conche, and on December 5, another was found at Chapel Arm, lying dead on the bottom, its arms waving slowly with the currents.

Scraps of squid seemed to be everywhere during the next few years. Bits were found at Newman's Cove on September 29, 1965; on October 8 more parts were found at Lance Cove. Another was caught somewhere off the coast later that month, and one washed up on a Springdale beach on November 24.

On November 9, 1966, a squid was found at Sweet Bay and on the 24th one was driven onto the landwash at Wild Cove, Fogo Island. Four days later Eddies Cove, on the Strait of Belle Isle, received its very own *Architeuthis dux*.

None were seen for a while, until, on November 18, 1971, Sunnyside received a malodorous blessing. On October 28, 1975, another came ashore at Bonavista; Lance Cove had its second squid arrive on November 21, 1977. There were stories of others turning up at various locales.

At Cottel Island, an entire squid presented itself near St. Brendan's on November 19, 1979, but unfortunately it was in several pieces. On November 14, 1981, a complete specimen turned up on the beach at Hare Bay, some 24 kilometres to the west; another washed up at Sandy Cove, Fogo Island, on October 30, 1982, but was in bad condition. Researchers thought this last one had probably engaged in battle with another cephalopod.

Among the latest is one that came ashore at Colliers in December 2004. Staff of Academy Canada in St. John's observed the recovery, and instructor Bob Richard said his intention had been to take some pictures and measurements. However, he decided to turn the creature over to Department of Fisheries and Oceans for examination.

Not overly large at 5.5 metres from tentacle-tip to tail, it drew some attention but was not the sensation of decades past. Today, the tiny community of Glovers Harbour (population of about 80) is proud of the fact that Canada Post produced a postage stamp in 2011 proclaiming their squid as one of Canada's premier roadside attractions.[27]

Today, the giant squid is Canada's only sea monster whose existence has been proven beyond a doubt. The once mythical and fearsome monster has become so ordinary that it is now treated as a mere curiosity and contemplated with a pronounced lack of enthusiasm; however, there are other creatures not so easily explained away.

1. Eric N. Simons, *Into Unknown Waters: John and Sebastian Cabot* (London: Dobson Books, 1964), 175–76.
2. Aaron Thomas, *The Newfoundland Journal of Aaron Thomas 1794*, ed. Jean M. Murray (London: Longmans, Green & Co. Ltd., 1968), 182–83.

3. Paul Hatcher & Nick Battey, *Biological Diversity: Exploiters and Exploited* (Sussex: John Wiley & Sons, 2011), 44.

4. A. E. Verrill, "The Cephalopods of the North-eastern Coast of America, Part I," *The Transactions of the Connecticut Academy of Sciences*, Vol. V, New Haven, CT (December 1879–March 1880), 83.

5. Frank Aubrey, "A Newfoundland Terror," *Fore's Sporting Notes and Sketches*, Vol. XIII (1896), 10–16. This note applies to the incidents described on pages 13–14.

6. Ibid.

7. Rev. Dr. Moses Harvey, LL.D., FRGS, FRCS. "How I Discovered the Great Devil-fish," *World Wide Magazine* (February 1873), 120; (1899), 732–40.

8. Verrill, "The Cephalopods of the North-eastern Coast," 124.

9. Horace Beck, *Folklore and the Sea* (Brattleboro, VT: Stephen Greene Press, 1973), 261.

10. Richard Ellis, *Monsters of the Sea* (Guilford, CT: Lyons Press, 2004), 122.

11. *The Canadian Illustrated News*, October 27, 1877.

12. John Robert Colombo, *Colombo's Book of Marvels* (Toronto: NC Press Ltd., 1979), 120–21.

13. A. E. Verrill, "Synopsis of the Cephalopoda of the Northeastern Coast of America," *American Journal of Science* (January to June, 1880), 285–87.

14. Bernard Heuvelmans, *In the Wake of the Sea-Serpents* (New York: Hill & Wang, 1968), 63–65.

15. Ellis, *Monsters of the Sea*, 128.

16. Verrill, "Synopsis of the Cephalopoda," 285–87.

17. Ibid.

18. H. M. Mosdell, *When Was That?* (St. John's: Trade Printers & Publishers, 1923), 64.

19. Verrill, "The Cephalopods of the North-eastern Coast," 123–130, 177–184.

20. *The Evening Mercury* (St. John's, NL), January 5, 1882.

21. *The Twillingate Sun*, January 17, 1891.

22. J. R. Smallwood, *The Best of the Barrelman* (September 1938), ed. William Connors (St. John's, NL: Creative Publishers, 1998), 29.

23. Ellis, *Monsters of the Sea*, 122.

24. Smallwood, *The Best of the Barrelman*, 29.

25. Heuvelmans, *In the Wake of the Sea-Serpants*, 123.

26. Ellis, *Monsters of the Sea*, 122.

27. Sue Hickey, "Canada Post celebrates the giant squid," *The Beacon* (Gander, NL), June 30, 2010, A8.

chapter

two

DEEP SeA SURVIVORS?

WHILE THE IDEA OF sea monsters and sea serpents is anathema to the scientific mind, men have believed in them for time immemorial. Though found around the globe with a good deal of frequency and recorded by virtually all cultures that have contact with the sea, these creatures have been reported in the greatest numbers in the higher and colder latitudes. Some accounts have been spectacular enough to draw the world's attention, such as Scotland's Great Orm of Loch Ness (better known as Nessie and a "lake monster") and our Pacific Coast's Caddy, both of which romp through the tabloids at irregular intervals.

The fourth-century Tyrrhenian poet Avienius based his *Ora Maritima* (*Sea Coasts*) on material from mariners' coasting directions. In it he told of a voyage by Carthaginian explorer Himilco (c. 600 bce) who had reported "monsters of the deep, and beasts swim amid the slow and sluggishly crawling ships."[1] Could these have been the mundane whales, squid, and seals with which we are familiar or, perhaps, the monsters of legend?

St. Brendan and his hardy crew, sailing the Atlantic in a mere currach, encountered the infamous Jasconius and other monsters.

ST. BRENDAN'S ATLANTIC VOYAGE more than a thousand years later is outlined in the *Navigatio Sancti Brendani*. Incredibly, Brendan was lucky enough to meet both St. Patrick and Judas Iscariot on that trip, the latter clinging to a rock while on probation from Hell. One hardly knows what to make of his tale of landing on Jasconius (sometimes called Aspidochelone), the gigantic fish of Irish traditions and legends that eternally and futilely labours to put its tail in its mouth. Upon this vast creature they beached their boat, the crew thinking it was an island, and here they celebrated Easter only to have the beast awaken in a pique when they lit a fire upon its back. While hastily making for their vessel, Brendan, apparently an inventive man of elastic conscience, breathlessly and belatedly explained that the mobile island was nothing less than Jasconius.[2]

Many have repeated the tale of Norsemen encountering a marine behemoth when they sailed from one of their few short-lived colonies here around 1,000 ce. It was said that on one occasion they fought off the monster Ednör until, in the final confrontation, the brute decided to investigate the Gulf of St. Lawrence. Evidently, it reached Montreal, but the Lachine Rapids stopped it from going farther.

A press release from amusement parks giant Six Flags, dated April 15, 2010, claimed this beast or its descendent showed up during construction of La Ronde's rollercoaster at Lac des Dauphins! On March 30, Dany Gauthier and Steve Saint-Louis, despite their shock, recorded the event with a cellphone camera. One Björn Sven Olafson, portrayed rather generously as an expert, confirmed the identity of the creature; accordingly, La Ronde named its new attraction for the infamous beast and promotion costs dropped significantly. Despite this, Six Flags was said to be conducting an inquiry into the incident. We continue to wait with bated breath for the results. In the meantime a ride called Serial Thriller, from the defunct AstroWorld south of Houston, Texas, has been installed at the park and renamed *Ednör – L'Attaque*, to take advantage of the event. At one point during the ride, passengers come near a substantial spout of water, ostensibly from Ednör, as described by the workers. It should be noted that Ednör, by an odd coincidence, happens to be "ronde" spelled backward.

Five hundred years after the Norsemen crossed it, the sea was still a vast expanse of mystery in which might be found diverse monsters and demons. The maps of John Cabot and other early explorers were replete with ill-conceived cultural detail and cautionary notes. Sea serpents, monsters, mer-creatures, and strange dog-faced people were shown in assorted territories, real and imagined. Cabot had apparently listened with great credulity to the yarns of old seagoing men; for instance, in the area of Iceland he depicted a great sea serpent destroying a ship and devouring her crew. Other ancient maps bore details just as lurid and fanciful, or more so, as a warning to those who might venture there.[3] No doubt the occasional discovery, from the Middle Ages through the eighteenth century, of fossilized bones of great prehistoric creatures did little to dispel these beliefs.

Even before the arrival of Europeans, the spirit world of the Beothuk included a powerful but unnamed monster from the sea. At least this was so according to Shanawdithit, thought to be the last of her race. William Epps Cormack, the first European to journey across Newfoundland, said the reason the Beothuk feared a sea monster is unclear, as her accounts were not easily understood and were translated only with great difficulty.[4]

ROUGHLY FOLLOWING CABOT'S PATH, Jacques Cartier sailed from Saint-Malo onto the Sea of Darkness, the Atlantic, in May 1534, hoping to reach the Orient. While Europeans had fished the Grand Banks for a considerable time (in fact Cartier himself had done so) few were willing to venture into the mysterious and menacing world beyond.

Twenty days of fine sailing put them on the Grand Banks, but this time Cartier pushed on into the Gulf of St. Lawrence and along Newfoundland's western shore where they were well aware of the risk of sea monsters. Thus, it was not unexpected when, somewhere

Jacques Cartier – contemplating the perils ahead?

in the Gulf, Cartier and his crew stumbled upon a giant, finned snake. He unkindly compared its motion to that of a caterpillar except for the use of the fins on its sides to propel itself through the water. Rashly, they attempted to capture the creature, but it was too fast and then, probably lucky for them, dove from sight – a splendid opportunity was lost.

Other well-known venturers got in on the act. Sir Humphrey Gilbert claimed Newfoundland for Queen Elizabeth on August 5, 1583. While returning to England on the minute *Squirrel* (nine tonnes) he spoke to the captain of the *Golden Hind* and his comforting words were recorded for posterity: "We are as near to Heaven by sea as by land." His vessel was not seen again and the *Golden Hind* was the only one of his five ships to complete the voyage. However, some time before his death he became somewhat more noted among his peers when he asserted that he had chanced upon a "lion-like sea monster with glaring eyes."[5] Some have suggested this was a giant squid, but the resemblance of these creatures to lions is remote at best.

Sightings of these seagoing anomalies have been recorded in detail; one may disregard suggestions that they were no more than a gam of whales, a pod of lesser *Cetacea* (i.e., dolphin or porpoise), or giant squid. One of the more usual forms observed is that of an immense serpent. Here a note of explanation is in order: Whereas "monster" means primarily a huge beast, "serpent" denotes a snakelike creature. A ribbonfish or oarfish, an eel or a sea cobra, could fall into this latter category.

Not only are these creatures seen in regions where visibility is often restricted by fog, rain, or snow, but they seem to prefer these places. Such are the coasts of Newfoundland and Labrador, particularly where the water is deep close to the shore, the tide runs hard, and the sea is greatly encumbered with off-lying reefs and ledges, many of which are covered with weeds.

Seventeenth-century English traveller *extraordinaire* John Josselyn has been criticized by some for his gullibility regarding what he saw and heard during his sojourn in North America. Still, his writings contain some of the earliest and most accurate information on the animals and plants of New England in that era, and they were lauded by Henry David Thoreau among others. On his visit he recorded an encounter settlers had with a sea serpent at Cape Ann in 1638:

> They told me of a sea serpent, or snake, that lay quoiled up like a cable upon the rock at Cape Ann; a boat passing by with English on-board, and two Indians, they would have shot the serpent, but the Indians dissuaded them, saying that if he were not killed outright, they would all be in danger of their lives...[6]

He further said that it had a head like that of a young lion. Recall Gilbert's lion-headed creature?

We can understand how, when brains are tired, weather is murky, and eyes ache with the strain of searching for danger, the wash of a tide rip over a weed-festooned rock, some debris in the water, or anything else unexpected could readily be taken for a sea monster. Indeed, it could take more than a little biological acumen to determine it was *not* one of these fearsome entities.

Another point to be borne in mind is that for various reasons basking sharks, turtles, whales, smaller *Cetacea*, cuttle-fish, and squid also tend to gather in these areas. All are common off Newfoundland and Labrador, and the lesser *Cetacea* are said to have a way of humping through the water, one after another, which in moderately poor visibility might briefly give the impression of a colossal undulating serpent.[7] Today many reported sightings of these unusual animals appear less than original, but they are nonetheless striking enough to excite the attention of our daily newspapers and the evening news.

Norwegian Hans Egede, a Lutheran missionary known as the Apostle of Greenland, noted naively that he regretted having seen no mermaids or other monsters such as he had expected on his second voyage to that great island. Of unchallenged integrity, he nevertheless recorded the appearance of another creature in a singular narrative. While sailing along the Greenland coast on July 6, 1734, northeast of Cape Chidley and en route to Godthaab on the Davis Strait, an uproar amongst the crew brought his attention to an object in the sea. His account reads:

> None of these sea-monsters have been seen by us, nor by any of our time that I could hear, save that most dreadful monster which showed itself on the surface of the water off our colony, in 64° N. latitude. This monster was of so huge a size that, coming out of the water, its head reached as high as the mainmast; its body was as bulky as the ship, and three or four times as long. It had a long, pointed snout, and spouted like a whale-fish; it had great broad paws; the body seemed covered with shell-work, and the skin was very ragged and uneven. The under part of its body was shaped like an enormous huge serpent; and when it dived again, under water, it plunged backwards into the sea, and so raised its tail aloft, which seemed a whole ship's length distant from the bulkiest part of its body.[8]

This creature may have been a form of primitive cetacean, which has since become extinct – the last recorded sighting of this sort was in 1848. A recent re-evaluation by some imaginative individual of this "most dreadful monster" suggests that it may have been a humpback whale (*Megaptera novaeangliae*), a North Atlantic right whale (*Eubalaena glacialis*), or one of the last remaining Atlantic grey whales (*Eschrichtius robustus*). All are unlikely candidates.

Contrasting reports of sea-dwellers of a similar gigantic size were not uncommon. A Mr. W. Lee told of a sea-snake he had

The colossal serpent seen by Hans Egede and depicted by Pastor Bing, who accompanied him on his voyage of 1734.

seen in the late 1700s in the Cabot Strait. More than 60 metres in length, its back was dark green and it stood up from the surface in "flexuous hillocks." In 1817, know-it-all Constantine S. Rafinesque said that it was the largest on record, as far as he knew, and suggested that it be called *Pelamis monstruosus*; he acknowledged, however, that if there are other species of equal size, it must then be called *Pelamis chloronotis*, or green-backed sea serpent.[9]

Rafinesque also reported a creature observed in the North Atlantic, *Octipos coccineus* (eight-gilled redfish), by the captain and crew of a ship from New York. It was reposing, coiled up near the surface of the water far from shore, in the summer of 1816. Rafinesque commented:

> It is very likely that it was a fish, and perhaps might belong to the same genus with the foregoing; I shall refer it thereto, with doubt, and name it Octipos Coccineus. – Entirely of a

bright crimson, head acute. Nothing further was added in the Gazettes where the account was given, except that its length was supposed to be about 40 feet [12 metres].[10]

At about the same time, the Moravian Brethren told a story heard from the Inuit at Nain concerning the Nennorluk. The natives claimed this to be a sea creature of considerable ferocity, a sort of amphibious bear that hunted and consumed seals, but was definitely not a polar bear. Each of its ears was big enough to make a large tent, and the creature ate human flesh whenever the opportunity arose. The Inuit, who had apparently seen it earlier that year, became quite exasperated if their reports were doubted.

This illustration has passed for the feared Nennorluk *of Labrador for some time, but it is likely an older and general representation of a sea monster by an unknown engraver.*

The Brethren and Inuit at Okak said they saw such a monster one evening in August 1786. It rose up to the height of a huge iceberg that stood at the mouth of the bay, exhibited its white back, and then plunged down in a smother of foam. The Inuit at once pronounced it to be the *Nennorluk*, but in an aside in his *History of Greenland*, David Crantz pointed out that the description was so vague that, "We may justly call in question whether they were not deceived by some tumbling ice-berg."[11] However, the legend of the *Nennorluk* was persistent and could not be easily ignored. Missionary Carl Gottfried Albrecht wrote from Nain on August 26, 1840, that the monster, which is white on the back like a polar bear, was seen that spring near the outer islands; that is, in the vicinity of Dog, Paul, and Kikkertavak Islands. At times it resembled a small island itself, but it could quickly sink from sight.

The *Nennorluk* did not swim, but rather walked on the sea bottom and could thus be seen only when it reached shallow water. It was said to make a thunderous noise; some claim to have heard the rocks on which it walked rattling as they turned over. Seals fled instantly when they detected one in their vicinity.

In the spring of 1847, Inuit once again reported the *Nennorluk*, this time near the steep and rocky cliffs of Cod Island at Cape Mugford. They said its sail-like ears protruded from the water with a space of one hundred paces between them. Choking with fright, they made all haste to gain the shore; afterward some asserted that its voice resembled low thunder, very harsh and unpleasant. This legendary creature is widely known among the Inuit. Celebrated anthropologist Knud Rasmussen even documented accounts from the Netsilik Inuit who live to the west of Hudson Bay.[12]

According to some Labrador residents, strange creatures were sighted at Hopedale Point years ago, on an unspecified date. In 1986, John Terriak of Nain related the story as it had been handed down to him by his father. Standing on the headland "near where Manasse Pijogge once lived," Inuit observed, just after spring breakup, an iceberg near the shore. To their great surprise and horror they saw the enormous eyes of mysterious creatures staring at them from *beneath* the ice. Their fear being much greater than their scientific curiosity, they hastily departed having gained no insight into its habits or even its appearance.[13] No other record has been found of the event.

Another unusual something was seen on the Labrador coast in 1878. *The Harbour Grace Standard* reported a sea monster at least as large as Egede's:

> "THE SEA SERPENT AGAIN." We have it on the authority of a gentleman whose name stands high in the estimation of his countrymen that the leviathan recently seen at Pack's Harbor completely eclipsed anything ever before witnessed in the waters which have our boats. Verily, truth is stranger than fiction.
>
> "Sir, – Under the description of the sea serpent sent me from Pack's Harbor Labrador. My brother says: I have no news to relate, only that a sea serpent or sea devil has been seen here two or three times this summer. He rose out of the water with a sharp point something like a marling-spike which increased in size until it was as large as the *Great Eastern*. Patrick Dawson saw him yesterday, and he said he could sail his boat under the curve described by the monster when he reared himself out of the water. The mast of his craft would not reach half way up to him. This is no romance – it is certain fact."
>
> That is all he says about him. I hope they will bring him home so that we may all see him. When he does may we and you, dear reader, be there to see.[14]

Perhaps many of these tales were told tongue in cheek, but if not, one day tourists cruising these waters in search of adventure may get the fright of their lives.

SS Anchoria, *an immigrant vessel, with ship's dory and crew in the foreground, at St. John's, October 1886.*

However, there was no apparent attempt at levity in 1879 when, according to *The New York Times*, one of these creatures was spotted on a Sunday evening. Anchor Line's SS *Anchoria* arrived at New York from Glasgow, and the newspaper related a tale told by Fourth Officer F. G. Rowell under the headline, "The Sea-serpent Shows Himself."

While on the Banks of Newfoundland the previous Thursday at 2:00 p.m., Rowell was on the bridge when he noticed a disturbance in the water about a kilometre off the port beam. Believing it was caused by a pod of porpoises, he nevertheless fetched his binoculars and was astonished to see the head and part of the body of a huge, rapidly swimming, serpent-like creature. He estimated its length to be at least equal to that of his 124-metre-long vessel.

Sections of its round, black body rose and fell as it propelled itself along the surface with a motion much like that of a snake (so he thought) its tail whipping the water in its wake to a lather. A disproportionally large mouth opened and closed frequently, each time expelling a gout of water. Its long tongue was visible at times, but no teeth could be seen. The brute was travelling in the same direction as, but faster than, the steamer. When it had a substantial lead on the ship, it submerged and was not seen again.

Several passengers on deck at the time saw the agitation of the sea and inquired of the second officer, a Mr. Baxter, what the cause was. He had but a quick glimpse of the thing before being obliged to return his attention to his duty; by the time he came back with his binoculars, it had vanished. Still, Baxter said he thought it to be some sort of sea monster and had complete confidence in Rowell's powers of observation and veracity. Rowell also had a particular interest in marine creatures and had studied them to some extent.[15]

Note that the description specifically mentions the extra-large and apparently toothless mouth, which would seem consistent with that of a creature that feeds on tiny sea creatures in the manner of the baleen whale. This unobtrusive detail, seldom mentioned in other cases, would appear to lend somewhat more credence to his story.

Chaplain Weiss of Lloyd's SS *Katie* gave a good report of a sea serpent he had seen on a journey from New York to Newcastle. At 9:00 p.m. on May 31, 1882, while passing just to the east of Newfoundland, he distinctly saw in the bright moonlight, a short distance away, a serpent about 55 metres long and six at its thickest part, "furnished with fins like lantern sails" (in all likelihood, lateen sails). Moreover, all the crew and passengers appeared on the deck to witness the wonderful sight.[16]

There have been at least a dozen sightings in the North Atlantic of what some have called a super-otter, primarily because of its shape and mammalian swimming motion. The general description is of a slender animal with a medium-length neck and long, tapering tail. Several vertical flexures had been noted, indicative of a mammal rather than a sort of fish or reptile.

Carbonear's Thomas Grant, owner of the fishing schooner *Augusta*, told of an encounter with the preternatural on August 11, 1888. The schooner's Captain Chidley had sent out six dories, one manned by Richard Grant and James Furlong. The two were busy hauling their trawl when a sudden commotion in the water caught their attention. Glancing up, they saw what they first thought to be a pod of dolphins but soon realized, to their great shock, were numerous parts of the same animal. It held its immense square head (some said sculpin-like, others, lizardlike) some five or six metres above the surface and fixed its huge eyes on the men. Its body, about six metres thick at the middle, was medium brown with darker stripes and had a huge fin.

Frightened half out their wits, they abandoned their gear and rowed furiously for the schooner. The 30-metre-long behemoth flattened its head against the surface and undulated through the water in hot pursuit. As it closed with the dory, one of the men, terror lending impetus to his actions, hurled a bait-tub at it, whereupon the beast turned its head, sniffed the tub, then quickly resumed its pursuit.

Catching up with the little boat, it lashed out with its tail but in doing so lost headway. A second bait-tub was thrown out in an attempt to distract it, but after a brief inspection, it again plunged after the fleeing dory and with even greater fury. By now, however, the men had reached safety, and as they clambered onto the schooner their frustrated pursuer submerged.

Later, when the fishermen had screwed up enough courage to make an attempt to retrieve their trawls, the creature reappeared. Once more it set out after a dory and attempted to destroy it with its great tail, but by now Captain Chidley, having

There were enough dangers in the business
without having to deal with grotesque monsters.

fetched a rifle, was ready. He fired one shot, and the beast sank instantly into the sea, probably more startled than injured, and was not seen again.

The *Augusta* returned to St. John's where the story appeared in the local newspapers. Some pundits thought it had been a giant squid, but this is another case where the captain and crew, familiar with squid of all sizes, should have the last word. Again, the fishermen said many parts of the creature appeared above the surface, implying that it had moved with a mammal-like up-and-down motion, but Chidley, contradictorily, said that it rippled as an eel would, that is from side to side.[17] This story was picked up by newspapers around the world, and shortly after, not surprisingly, a similar creature was reported off the coast of Massachusetts. Unfortunately, however, no corroborating evidence of *Augusta*'s exciting encounter can be found.

Antoon Cornelis Oudemans, Doctor of Zoology and Botany and Director of the Royal Zoological and Botanical Society at The Hague, was probably the most renowned scientist ever to take on sea serpent cases; he had a huge influence on later researchers. In 1892 his book, *The Great Sea Serpent*, was published; in it he suggested that many reports were best accounted for as a previously unknown giant, long-necked pinniped; that is, a member of the seals' extended family which includes the walrus and sea lion.

A measure of how seriously sea monsters were taken a century ago may be gauged by the following account taken from *The New York Times* of February 5, 1887:

> Bullard and King's new steamship *Umtali* was some 300 miles [483 kilometres] north of Cape Verde when it encountered a sea monster...Chief Officer C. A. Powell was in charge of the bridge when he saw a strange object about 300 yards [236 metres] away. It appeared to be a huge and "slimy" serpent, about the size of a whale in circumference, with several pairs of short fins 20 feet [6 metres] apart. Around 90 feet [27 metres] of its considerable length could be seen above the water.
>
> Several passengers on deck took turns viewing the creature through binoculars and Powell clearly saw the beast's mouth, its two-metre-long jaw armed with huge teeth, open and shut. It looked like a huge conger eel in shape and colour, the skin underneath being white...Captain Cringle came onto the bridge and seeing the object of their attention he changed the ship's course toward it. At this, the serpent headed directly toward them until it was about 50 metres off, then changed its direction and swam from sight.[18]

Many newspaper reports poured ridicule upon Captain Cringle, and he refused to discuss the subject for years afterward. This account is somewhat more credible than many, as the calm observer delivered a description giving greater and more reasonable details than usual.

Nova Scotian Howard Blackburn is famed for going astray from the Gloucester fishing schooner *Grace L. Fears*, Captain Alec Griffin, on Burgeo Bank with Newfoundlander Thomas Welch on January 25, 1883. Welch died, and Blackburn survived four days and nights in sub-zero temperatures, though he lost all his fingers. While Welch rested in the Burgeo cemetery, Blackburn became even more famous by twice sailing across the Atlantic, single-handedly and fingerless.

In 1931, Blackburn told author and historian Edward R. Snow that on July 1, 1901, while making one of these crossings in his boat the *Great Republic*, he had seen a real sea serpent on the eastern edge of the Newfoundland Banks. He concluded that it was a "baby" sea serpent as it was only about five metres long and had a large fish or a small turtle in its mouth. The tail and parts of the body that he could see appeared to be smooth and of a light lead colour. He explained that he had gotten within a couple of metres of it, and despite having no fingers, he had tried to lasso and bring it back to "make those at home, sit up."[19]

A similar beast was spotted off England in 1912 by those on-board the German ship *Kaiserin Augusta Victoria*. Captain Ruser's brief description said it was about six metres long and a half-metre thick.

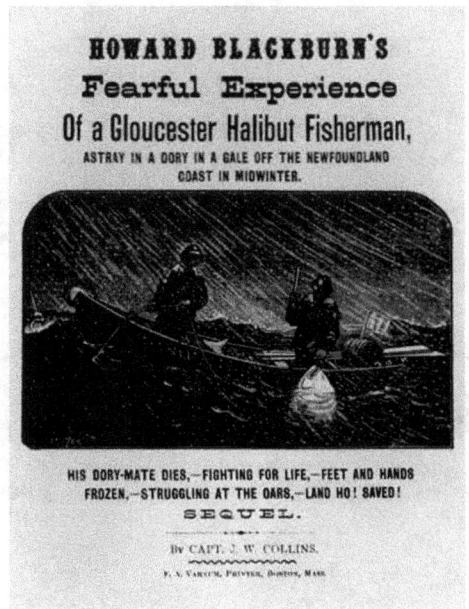

HOWARD BLACKBURN'S
Fearful Experience
Of a Gloucester Halibut Fisherman,
ASTRAY IN A DORY IN A GALE OFF THE NEWFOUNDLAND COAST IN MIDWINTER.

HIS DORY-MATE DIES,—FIGHTING FOR LIFE,—FEET AND HANDS FROZEN,—STRUGGLING AT THE OARS,—LAND HO! SAVED!
SEQUEL.

By CAPT. J. W. COLLINS.

F. A. VARCUM, PRINTER, BOSTON, MASS.

Howard Blackburn's experience made him a hero long before his solo ocean voyages.

Back on the Grand Banks, a more impressive and kindlier looking monster appeared to those on board the Allan Line's passenger vessel SS *Corinthian*, Captain Tannock, on August 30, 1913. While on passage from London to Montreal, the second officer, a Mr. G. Batchelor, was on watch at 4:30 a.m., and scanning the horizon, he spied an object about a kilometre or so distant and dead ahead. He supposed it to be a fishing boat lying end-on to his ship. In the dense fogs of the fishing banks, sailors frequently became separated from their schooners, and many had to wait days to be picked up, if they were picked up at all. Having such an event in mind, he was surprised when it suddenly submerged, and his first thought was that the boat had sunk.

Allan Line's SS Corinthian.

However, when *Corinthian* approached the area, a more surprising sight presented itself. Fifty or sixty metres away there emerged from the water an immense, flat, diamond-shaped head with a wide mouth, long fin-like ears, and great mild, liquid blue eyes holding no hint of ferocity. There followed a giraffe-like neck about six metres long – its short, water-smoothed fur of a "giddy yet good" light brown-yellow with spots of a darker hue, led to it being aptly dubbed the "sea giraffe." It had a seal-like body, about the same length as its neck, and its bifurcate tail formed a pair of "daddles" (i.e., flippers or fins). Batchelor concluded that the three horned fins on its bony head were probably for defence and attack or for "ripping things up." The monster took its time examining the ship and occupants; its head swaying so easily and rhythmically on its supple neck that Batchelor said it was as if it were "on a ball bearing."

Expressing curiosity, it swam rapidly toward the ship with pronounced vertical undulations and inspected them closely, the large long-suffering eyes appearing to display a "surprised, injured, and fearful state." When satisfied it slowly submerged and was not seen again.[20]

This may be one of the more common varieties of sea monster, as it seems to be a version of the 30-metre-long dark-brown creature seen by the officers of RMS *Athenian* between the Canary Islands and the Cape Verde Islands 50 years earlier.[21] Heuvelmans placed such creatures within the classification of "merhorse" in 1965, and gave it the ready-to-hand name of *Halshippul olaimagni*.

Not surprisingly, the unpleasantness we know as the First World War probably disturbed many sea-dwellers. On July 30, 1915, the German submarine *U-28* torpedoed the British freighter *Iberian*, Captain T. B. Jago, 15 kilometres south-by-west of Fastnet, Ireland. The freighter was en route from Manchester to Boston with general cargo; seven died when it rapidly went down, stern first. As the crew of the *U-28* watched, there was a large explosion that sent water and wreckage into the air. Kapitänleutnant Freiherr Georg-Günther von Forstner entered the encounter in his log:

> Moments later the hull of the Iberian disappeared...there was a violent explosion, which shot pieces of debris – among them a gigantic aquatic animal – out of the water to a height of approximately 80 feet [24 metres]...At that moment I had with me in the conning tower six of my officers...Simultaneously we all drew one another's attention to this wonder of the seas, which was writhing and struggling among the debris...all of us agreed that it resembled an aquatic crocodile, which was about 18 metres, with four limbs resembling large webbed feet, a long, pointed tail and a head which also tapered to a point. Unfortunately we were not able to take a photograph, for the animal sank out of sight after ten or fifteen seconds.[22]

Aboard the accompanying *U-20*, the equally restrained Kapitänleutnant Werner-Lowisch matter-of-factly reported:

> Saw a sea serpent at 10 p.m., without possibility of doubt. The creature had a longish head, scales like a crocodile's, and legs with proper feet. The mate saw him, but when the captain came up from below, the monster had vanished... [23]

This one is particularly difficult to explain away as U-boat commanders were not given to flights of fancy or delusions. If Herren von Forstner and Werner-Lowisch did witness such a thing, it took the former nearly 20 years to bring it to light. In 1933, von Forstner wrote an article regarding the Loch Ness monster for a German newspaper and brought up his own experience at that time.

Another truly extraordinary case reported in the north-east Atlantic may never have taken place at all. Near the end of the First World War, the German torpedo attack boat *UB-85* was

Von Forstner's alligator-like monster.

destroyed by the steam drifter HMS *Coreopsis II*. On April 30, 1918, the British crew were surprised and pleased to find the submarine sitting on the surface for no apparent reason. Her crew of 34 were taken off and she was sent to the bottom by gunfire.

The U-boat's commander, 32-year-old Kapitänleutnant Günther Krech, explained that they had surfaced to recharge their batteries and were taken unawares by a strange beast. The submarine had rocked abruptly, as the creature dragged its considerable weight onto the starboard bow, then listed badly.

Krech described it as having large eyes set in a horny sort of skull, a small head, and teeth that glistened in the moonlight. Every man on watch began firing his sidearm at it but it grasped the forward gun-mount and refused to let go (this would suggest that it had something *with which to grasp*). Fearing the open hatch would dip below the waterline and thus flood his vessel, Krech ordered their barrage continued until the creature dropped back into the sea. During the struggle the forward deck plating was badly damaged and as a result they were unable to submerge. Though it is true that *UB-85* was sunk by *Coreopsis II* and Krech was real, no corroborating evidence for this tale of a sea monster has been found. R. H. Gibson and Maurice Prendergast, in their excellent chronicle, *The German Submarine War, 1914-1918*, describe the action but make no mention of a sea-creature. There is, of course, the possibility that "reports" of the monster were generated, completely free of any influence by participants of the naval action, sometime afterward.[24]

Both these tales involve U-boats and colossal denizens of the sea, and there is no incontrovertible evidence that either actually took place. Many doubters have stepped forward, and rightly so, some going so far as to say there was never a ship named *Iberian*. It would be unfair to pass on outright falsehoods, but according to HMS *Stationery Office, British Merchant Shipping Losses of WWI*, SS *Iberian* was built by Sir James Laing & Sons, Sunderland, England, in 1900, and at the time of her loss, was owned by F. Leyland & Company of Liverpool. *Coreopsis*, *UB-85*, and *U-28* were certainly very real and much information on them is available.

This particular creature did not answer any earlier descriptions of sea monsters, but as we shall see, there appear to be many varieties. In 1922, another curiosity put in an appearance off British Harbour, Random Island. Colossal sea dwellers reported to be from 12 to 20 metres long attacked the settlement's fishing boats. The men were

Kapitänleutnant Günther Krech of U-28.

sufficiently terrified to forego the fishery for some time, refusing to go out to the grounds, and several boats narrowly escaped being swamped in attempts to do so.

According to *The Evening Telegram* of September 16, a large group of these brutes, of which no description was given, appeared off the coast and remained despite an expedition organized by the local communities to capture or disperse them. On September 19, a headline in *The New York Times* blared: "'SEA MONSTERS' ATTACK NEWFOUNDLAND BOATS; Scare Fishermen From Grounds – Expedition to Capture Them Is Planned."[25] Evidently, the invasion was reported to the Department of Marine and Fisheries by the telegraph operator at British Harbour, but the results of his effort are unknown. Despite the lack of a description, in light of the events of August 17, 2010 (when a gam of killer whales was seen attacking a minke whale in Trinity Bay), one wonders if the monsters might

Could these be the monsters seen by Trinity fishermen in 1922?

have been the orca we all know. Orcas were also seen along the Southern Shore that summer and again in the summer of 2011, while others have been reported on the Grand Banks and in the Strait of Belle Isle.

In fact, according to the CBC News, one of these rammed a boat off Newfoundland on the weekend of July 12–13, 2008. Amy Chislett and three friends were off Cape St. Francis when someone brought their attention to what Chislett said was "the biggest, blackest fin, I'd ever seen," headed straight for them. They braced themselves – there was a resounding crash and the perturbed mammal took its leave.

Sometimes a report from a witness was not forthcoming, nor was one really needed to attest to the fear resulting from the experience. Otto Kelland (Constable Kelland in the 1930s, one of our more celebrated sons) investigated the conditions of able-bodied relief for the Department of Public Health and Welfare. In one settlement, he obtained the list of relief recipients, and as he reviewed it, the relieving officer did so as well. The latter offhandedly remarked that it was too bad that one particular man was on the dole.

When questioned, the relieving officer explained that three years ago the fisherman was a proud independent man and a hard worker. Then one day he had gone out in his motor-dory taking along two tubs of baited trawl. Toward noon, a half-dozen men on the wharf saw his boat running into the harbour, throttle wide open. This did not surprise them, but they *were* surprised when he ran his dory past the wharf and full tilt up onto the beach.

The man stumbled from his boat in a state of shock, perspiring, shaking, and unable to speak. Taken to his house he lay down and his unnerved wife asked him what had happened. He gave no details and said that he had not been hurt but had "got a terrible fright."

Since his trawls were missing, it was assumed he had set them out and later, while checking them, something frightened him out of his wits. When pressed, he exclaimed that he would never tell anyone as they would not believe him anyway. Further, he swore he was done with fishing for good. Shortly after, he sold his dory and all his fishing gear and steadfastly refused to set foot in a boat again. Having no choice but to accept the dole, he was interviewed by Kelland who portrayed him as a deep-chested and broad-shouldered man, quiet and polite, more than 5'9" tall, with massive arms. Kelland noted that it must have been a horrifying experience that forced such a man to abandon the life he loved. It is said that he later told the parish priest of the affair, but that individual took his secret to the grave.[26]

In August 1936, *The Boston Herald* carried a tale of a sea monster off the coast of Nova Scotia. Datelined August 11, Liverpool, it gave no description of the beast. Then came a report from St. John's that was printed on Wednesday, August 19. As with many descriptions, the monster's size may have been exaggerated since the headline read, "150-Foot Sea Monster Seen off Newfoundland." The item continued:

> The Newfoundland natural resources department announced today that fishermen on the west coast of Newfoundland had reported a second appearance of what they said was a 150-foot [46 metres] sea monster. The department said fishermen at Port au Port sent messages to the department last week saying the reported monster has scared boats away from fishing grounds in that vicinity.[27]

But clearly this one was small fry, because on Friday another account from St. John's made the news. This time the monster was *truly* a monster and the story ran:

> Fishermen Say Head Stuck 60 Feet [18 metres] Out of Water. Newfoundland fishermen told vivid – but unconfirmed – tales tonight of a sea monster on the west coast that stuck its head 60 feet [18 metres] out of the water and

snorted blue vapour from its nostrils. Sharp-eyed fishermen produced a collective picture of the monster like this: At least 200 feet [61 metres] long and 18 feet [5.5 metres] in diameter, eyes as big as an enamel sauce pan and spaced two feet apart; a mane larger than that of any horse. The fishermen even claimed the monster was so big it set up waves that rocked fishing boats and for days no boat ventured to sea...

This was a spectacular account but, whatever the thing was, it was not reported again. Even so, on August 28 *The Boston Evening Transcript* ran a piece, in apparent disbelief, asking, "Sea Serpent or Squid?"

Is it not rather late in the summer for the hotel-keepers of Newfoundland to try to attract visitors to her rocky coast by sending out stories that the largest sea monster of all time is disporting itself in the icy waters of Port au Port Bay on the west coast of the island? Should we give more credence to the account because it can serve no ulterior purpose, cannot bring summer folks to the island in shoals to gaze upon the creature?...In northern latitudes sea serpents invariably appear off shore before mid-July. They come up at dusk to gambol in the moonshine and sink to the abysmal ooze at dawn. That is why they are rarely and dimly seen. By the end of August they are well on their way South to more genial waters.[28]

In apparent disregard of this attempt at levity, some strange things did reside in our waters. In 1937, Newfoundland Ranger Matthew Davis reported that two fishermen of Tack's Beach had to run their rapidly sinking boat ashore after being attacked by an enormous fish with "teeth like arrow heads." Davis' brief report reads:

On Saturday last whilst Joseph Warren and his hired man

were hauling their cod net a huge brown-backed fish seized the keel forward and almost overturned the boat. Letting go the stem, the fish seized the keel amidships and then near the stern, lifting the boat so much out of the water that the bow went under and a lot of water was shipped. [29]

The ranger said that, once on shore, the two checked the bottom of their boat and found the keel had been twisted nearly free of the timbers and had three immense broken teeth embedded in it. These were carefully removed and sent to Dr. N. L. McPherson of the Fisheries Research Office in St. John's, but the culprit was never identified.

Around the same time, George Budgell, Hudson's Bay Company manager at Rigolet, his son Leonard, and Captain John Blake of the 20-tonne motor sloop *Fort Rigolet* were loading that vessel with supplies and mail for the post at North West River. The tide was out and in the narrows of Groswater Bay (now Hamilton Inlet) the current can easily run at five or six knots. Budgell saw, about 400 metres offshore, what he thought was a large black log being carried by the tide. He was astonished when the log raised a huge head and focussed a pair of enormous and baleful eyes on him that looked "deadly human." Reptilian faces are not known for their range of expression, and if this monstrosity had vicious intent there is no reason why it should not have attacked. It stared at the men for about 15 seconds, then submerged.

Budgell said the head was the size of that of a square-flipper or bearded seal (*Erignathus barbatus*), on a half-metre-long neck. The creature itself was about five metres long, as big around as a pork barrel, and when it dove it showed three humps. "If ever I put up an earnest prayer during my sinful career it was that I might have my rifle by me at that moment," Budgell said fervently.[30]

This multi-humped type of sea monster has also been identified by Heuvelmans. His description gives it an elongated body of up to 35 metres long and from three to five metres in diameter. Dull green to dark-brown or black on top, its throat and underside are pure white. The skin, though usually smooth, is sometimes mentioned as rough, and scales have been occasionally observed. Its ovoid head, flat on top, has eyes about 15 centimetres in diameter and a broad snout; its slender neck has one or two white stripes along each side. With its pair of frontal flippers, it swims with an undulating motion similar to that of a caterpillar. Though there had been frequent sightings at one time, it became much rarer in the North Atlantic after 1900.

The commonplace sea monster went by the boards in the 1940s when there was a series of odd sightings in Placentia Bay. Fisherman Abe Brinston of Arch Cove said he had never paid much attention to the stories of strange beasts in Newfoundland waters until he met one. While working on his boat's engine, he felt the vessel rise in the water. He automatically stood up, then

The caption on this unknown artist's rendering reads, "Taken from life as appeared in Gloucester Harbour, August 23, 1817." The creature was said to be more than 20 metres in length and swam rapidly.

nearly had a heart attack. There, peering over the gunwale, was "nothing less than the Devil himself! It tried to climb into my boat and was grasping the gunwale with a monstrous set of claws!"

The beast was dragging the boat under when Brinston grabbed a gaff and began thumping it about the head and claws. Finally, the thing let go and submerged, and Brinston speedily headed home, knowing full well that no one would believe him.

Still, he told family and friends of his ordeal while they stared at him, unbelievingly. Their disbelief was suspended next day when fisherman Clayton Stacey of nearby Sound Island met the same creature, or at least a member of its family, as the descriptions matched exactly. Stacey, however, had a gun and took a shot at it. Though the creature let go of the boat and submerged, leaving a smear of blood in the water, Stacey did not think he had seriously injured it. For the next month or so fishermen were not only careful, but armed.

Next, it appeared near New Harbour (could this have been North Harbour?) where men fishing at the mouth of the river saw it approaching and hurriedly left the water. One of them told a reporter from *The Evening Telegram*, "It was as big around as a puncheon and an awful length." It tried to pull itself up on the rocks close to shore, but each time it slipped back into the water.[31]

The strange creature was frequently called the devilfish; some, referred to rather generously as experts, claimed, without a shred of evidence, that it was likely a giant squid. This, despite the fact that every Newfoundland fisherman knows a squid – giant or midget – when he sees one.

Shortly after World War II, the noted Dr. Nathan M. Budgell, VS, DVM, late of the Royal Canadian Army Medical Corps, arrived home in Springdale. His mother, Mrs. Susan (Peter) Budgell, told him that she and others had often seen a huge snakelike creature in the waters of Halls Bay. Apparently,

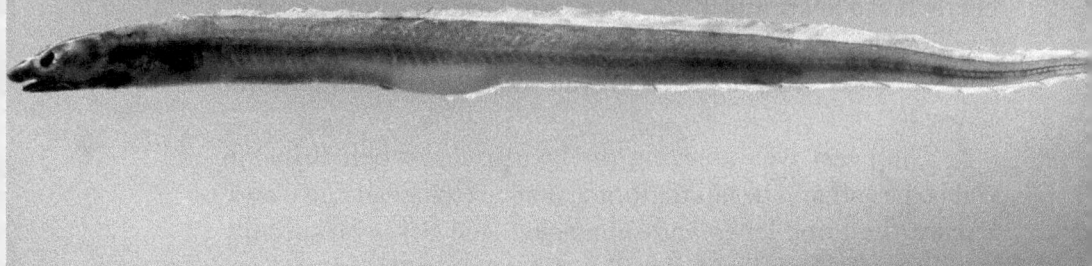

A conger eel. Imagine one 20 metres long and weighing 160 kilograms.

the beast lifted its head high above the surface and was some 18 to 20 metres long.

Dr. Budgell said locals called it a conger eel and thought that it solved the puzzle of sea serpents. These eels seldom reach three metres in length and most are much smaller; however, the largest on record was a giant of nearly 160 kilograms caught in a net off Westmann Island, Iceland. The knowledgeable doctor was sure that, whatever they saw, it was not a conger eel as we know it, and its identity remains a mystery.[32]

On July 31, 1954, a fisherman from The Battery reported a sea monster. No further description is available, but it was obviously a creature of some size and distinction as it was mentioned by J. R. Smallwood in his *Book of Newfoundland*. Smallwood did not trouble to check further, however, so any worthwhile information went unrecorded.[33]

It was not until 1966 that there was another significant sighting. It involved two highly dependable witnesses who went on to become world-famous for their exploits at sea: 28-year-old Captain John Ridgway and 26-year-old Sergeant Charles "Chay" Blyth, both of Britain's renowned Royal Parachute Regiment.

Having left Cape Cod, Massachusetts, for Ireland in their boat *English Rose III* on June 4, they were just east of the Flemish Cap on July 25. Early that morning Blyth was sleeping and

Ridgway was pulling inattentively at the oars when his rowing was suddenly interrupted. He wrote:

> I was shocked to full wakefulness by a swishing noise to starboard. I looked out into the water and suddenly saw the writhing, twisting shape of a great creature. It was outlined by the phosphorescence in the sea as if a string of neon lights were hanging from it. It was an enormous size, some thirty-five or more feet [nearly 11 metres] long, and it came towards me quite fast. I must have watched it for some ten seconds. It headed straight at me and disappeared right beneath me. I stopped rowing. I was frozen with terror at this apparition. I forced myself to turn my head to look over to port side. I saw nothing, but after a brief pause I heard a most tremendous splash. I am not an imaginative man, and I searched for a rational explanation. Chay and I had seen whales and sharks, dolphins and porpoises, flying fish – all sorts of sea creatures but this monster in the night was none of these. I reluctantly had to believe that there was only one thing it could have been – a sea serpent.[34]

On September 3, the two washed up on Ireland's Aran Islands, 92 days after their departure. Today they are John Ridgway, MBE, and Sir Charles Blyth, CBE, BEM.

It has even been said that we once had our very own preserved sea serpent: it was found in the nets of a Portuguese fishing boat off the coast of Newfoundland in 1989. Partially decomposed and with its fins badly torn, it was thought to have been struck by a passing ship. That, or it had been preserved in ice for thousands or millions of years and had only recently thawed out. Who preserved it, or where it is now, is unknown.

June 10, 1992, had started out as most days did for Baine Harbour's Jones brothers, Felix, Eugene, and Peter. It was foggy with a light easterly wind as they set out in their six-metre longboat to haul their gillnets. An hour later they came upon the small buoy marking the spot, barely visible in the fog.

They had a fair catch of about 11 quintals (550 kilograms) when, shortly after noon, the fog lifted and they took a lunch break. Afterward, with the engine off and the radio silent, they began cleaning fish. Abruptly, the serenity was shattered. Felix and Eugene watched incredulously as an enormous "greeny-black" creature flung itself at the boat, directly toward Peter who was looking the other way.

They simultaneously screamed a warning, but Peter never did see what was coming. The creature's capacious tooth-filled mouth came down on the starboard side of the boat's plywood housing, and the whole affair turned upside down. All three were thrown into the frigid water, and Peter lost sight of his brothers. Finally, the two emerged from beneath the capsized boat and clutched the hull, concerned that their catch might serve as bait for whatever had wrecked them.

At home, Tom Jones was worried when his sons had not shown up two hours after they were expected. Anxious, as it would soon be dark and finding them afterward would be near impossible, he and neighbour, Melvin Murphy, began a search. Just at dusk they found the missing boat and took the men to the hospital at Burin; only Felix required attention, having gotten a severe knock on the head.[35]

The brothers still do not know what attacked them, but marine experts who examined the marks left in the plywood by its teeth think this sea monster may have been a great white shark. Though they can be up to six metres long, they are also very rare this far north and are seldom, if ever, greeny-black. But what else could it have been?

Also, in 1992, Bay L'Argent fisherman John Hardiman told of an encounter with a perplexing denizen of the sea some years earlier. His revelation appeared in *The Telegram*:

> "It was the y'er the ice floes come further south than we've ever witnessed and flowed up into Fortune Bay," said John Hardiman, 66. "It was exactly the same as them fellas

described it. But I never seen its head, that was beneath the water. I did see its big long tail, more like those dinosaurs you see on TV. That's what it looked like to me."[36]

Such incidents are not as uncommon as many might think. A study in the United States listed more than 600 sightings and reported that more than half were not obvious hoaxes or cases of mistaken identity. Charles Bungay of Little Bay East, Fortune Bay, has no doubt about what he saw on May 4, 1997. It was a sea monster. "It was frightening," Bungay exclaimed in a masterpiece of understatement. "I shook for about five or six hours afterwards. I've never witnessed anything like it in my life."

Dr. Jon Lien, a marine biologist at Memorial University, was reluctant to speculate on what Bungay might have seen, but he ruled out a humpback whale, large basking shark, or giant squid. Lien said that after he had received a full description he was more inclined to think along the lines of a creature comparable to *Cadborosaurus*, supposedly seen on numerous occasions along the coast of British Columbia. He added, "Maybe we've just discovered the east coast version of that so-called sea monster, I don't know."

Memorial's archivist, Dr. Philip Hiscock, dismissed the fisherman's monster as a giant squid, but Bungay bridled at that: "I knows it wasn't a giant squid and I knows it wasn't a shark and I knows it wasn't a seal," he snorted. "I've seen all this before. I mean I've never seen a giant squid, only pictures of it, but I knows that wasn't no giant squid."

Paul LeBlond, an authority on marine cryptozoology, was contacted by a friend who thought he had recognized the description of the unfamiliar creature in *The Telegram*. He was of the opinion that, again, it was likely a creature related to those of Canada's west coast.[37]

In the spring of 2000, Bonavista resident Bob Crewe became a firm believer in sea monsters. While driving alone along the Cape Bonavista shore on the morning of April 5, Crewe saw a creature unlike anything he had ever seen before. The beast, nine or ten metres long, lay in the water, hardly moving. Crewe stopped his truck at the edge of the cliff overlooking the ocean in Dungeon Provincial Park, near the rock formation known as the Viking. He said that at first he

The Viking, Dungeon Provincial Park.

imagined it was another rock, but he knew no rock was supposed to be there. He sounded his truck's horn, and the animal raised its head from the water, displaying nearly two metres of neck.

Crewe said that from what he could see of the beast in the ruffled water, it was similar to a huge snake with "a snout." It left and swam off toward the lighthouse, its head still above the surface and tilted forward. It appeared to make much use of its body when swimming and was deceptively fast.

Dr. Lien said the creature could have been a large piece of driftwood, a group of dolphins or seals, or a giant squid. Crewe, a native of the area, is certainly bright enough to recognize a seal or a stick when he sees one. He retorted that what he saw was nothing as simple as that. "It wasn't a giant squid. I know that for sure," he said. "I wasn't close enough to see scaly skin or eyes or any detail like that. All I know is that it was a strange creature, and it's a big ocean that could contain a lot of strange things we've never seen."[38]

Under the headline "A Strange Sea Creature was Seen Off Cape," *The Globe and Mail* reported:

> If residents of Bonavista have seen Newfoundland's answer to the Loch Ness monster, they're not saying. So far, local man Bob Crewe is the only one to go public with his account of a strange sea creature off Cape Bonavista. Another resident, who asked not to be identified, told a radio station there are others who will admit privately to seeing something unusual. But they're not prepared to go on the record.[39]

The Dungeon itself, a collapsed sea cave near Bonavista on what is locally known as the Backside, is about three kilometres south of the Cape Bonavista lighthouse. This innocuous-looking hole is said to be one of the many places around the world to be cursed or blessed by the presence of these outlandish creatures. In an article titled "Ogopogo the Chameleon," Benjamin

Radford discusses sea serpents and various lake monsters and declares the following: "I encountered one such area on the coast of Newfoundland – a huge, dark, unusual sinkhole near a rocky cliff that had washed out two holes toward the ocean. It is called The Dungeon, and is said to be home to sea monsters."[40]

At times, possible sea monsters wash onto our shores, but the remains are in such states of decomposition that it is difficult to say what they may have been. The term "globster" was first used by naturalist Ivan T. Sanderson, in 1962, to describe a carcass that had washed up on the shores of Tasmania two years earlier. It was said to have no visible eyes, no defined head, and no apparent bone structure. Over the years, other globsters appeared, and when an unidentifiable mass was found washed ashore near North Peltry Cove (some 20 kilometres west-southwest of St. Bernard's, Fortune Bay, in 2002) it immediately became the "blobster."

Here, fisherman Ed Hodder had a shack in which he could stay close to his nets. On August 2, he spotted what he thought was an overturned dory on shore and put his boat about for the beach. It was not a dory, but an unidentifiable something or other. Others came to see and called it simply "the monster." One fisherman commented, "We people have never seen the likes of it before; we never."

Hodder estimated its weight to be three or four tonnes and its length about seven metres. There was a skeleton of sorts, at least a backbone and ribs, though it was difficult to tell the head from the tail. There was no hint of limbs, but two fleshy flaps on each side could have been fins. Bystanders were baffled by what appeared to be a coat of coarse white hair about 15 centimetres long. An exasperated Hodder declared, "The hair is the biggest puzzle. What's hair doing on any kind of our fish?"

The Dungeon, Dungeon Provincial Park, Bonavista.

Some indication of the stench is the fact that it made some fishermen sick (a decidedly difficult thing to do), and even seagulls avoided the place. Among the interested fishermen was Charles Bungay, of Little Bay East, who saw the monster in 1997. While he could not say what it was, he did say that it looked as if it might be the remains of a similar beast.

An interesting aspect of the transformation from whale to a puzzling carcass is that, as the former decomposes, fibrous tissue takes on the appearance of a white hairy coat. According to William Shatner's *Weird or What?*, Dr. Garry Stenson of the federal Department of Fisheries and Oceans has since explained that the blobsters have proven to be made up mostly of collagen, a connective tissue with the tensile strength of steel. Since the washed up substance contains no trace of innards or bones, Matthew Wedel, professor of anatomy, has theorized that when a whale dies this tough skin may float about for years while identifiable remnants fall out and drop to the bottom. This leaves the skin to fray to a hairy leftover, wash up on the beach, and baffle even the most knowledgeable of witnesses. It was all very intriguing, but Dr. Stenson finally had the monster's DNA analyzed at the Genetics, Evolution, and Molecular Systematics Laboratory at Memorial University. On August 16, it was pronounced to be the mouldering remains of a sperm whale,[41] perhaps to the disappointment of some.

More recently, on the afternoon of February 18, 2010, Warrick Lovell, of McIver's, saw what he thought was a dead seal brought in by the tide at Lower Cove. Later, when he went to check on his boat, he strolled over for a closer look. Lovell was startled to see the unfamiliar remains of something that had once been alive; he had no idea what. It was certainly not a seal. About three metres of the five-metre-long creature was mostly tail; it also had what appeared to be a flipper-like appendage on its right side, was headless, and showed evidence of trauma, possibly caused by some predator.

When word of Lovell's find got around, inquisitive residents began showing up for a look. Basil Park said, "I didn't know what to think of it. I've lived here all my life and never seen anything like it."

"It's got hair on it in spots; I couldn't tell what it was," Park marvelled. "There's fishermen here who fished all their lives and they couldn't tell you."

John Lubar of the Department of Fisheries and Oceans said the Corner Brook office receives a number of calls from residents around the region each year reporting seals in brooks or to have rotting carcasses of whales or other animals removed from a shoreline. However, reports of unknown marine fauna washing up are rare.[42] In early April, the mystery was solved when Memorial University investigators revealed that they were 99 percent certain that this monster was the remains of a blue whale.

This story evidently awakened memories in John Marsh of Lower Lance Cove. In March 2010, *The Telegram* received an unusual letter from him relating an experience he had the year before.

Marsh, with about 60 years of fishing experience under his belt, was called upon by his son and nephew in 2009 to help free a whale from one of their traps. To his amazement, it was something he had never before seen or, for that matter, even imagined. The first indication that they had something unusual was when a head, with camel-like lips and rounded teeth, emerged from the water on the end of a three-metre-long neck; at the other end was a three-pointed tail. Marsh said its pretty blue-green skin was as smooth as glass while whales, on the other hand, have scratches and even barnacles on them – but this thing was perfectly clean ("like 'e just come from a washer," Marsh elaborated). This led him to believe it may have lived in or near fresh water. Thinking it was going nowhere in a hurry, Marsh left for an appointment with a doctor, perhaps unreasonably some may think, and by the time he returned it had sunk.[43]

Jack Lawson, a marine mammal research scientist with the

Department of Fisheries and Oceans, said he would have been elated had Marsh taken a tissue sample for a DNA test as he had never heard of anything having such an admixture of features. He added that it might have been a whale or other creature mutilated by the propellers of a ship or something in a state of decomposition. Lawson thought that perhaps Marsh, too, had seen a *Cadborosaurus*, but after being given a description and shown an artist's rendering of that creature, the fisherman said it was not what he had seen.[44]

This finds us back where we began with possibly less of an idea where "monsters of the deep" come from, where they go, or what they are. Unlike the giant squid, these creatures remain a mystery. Can science actually disprove the firm convictions of those who believe they have encountered something, like those creatures that decorate the maps of old, that dwell beyond the margins of the known world? Or are we best left to contemplate the "perhaps" of it all? Such monsters are not the only possible "others" out there; there are sea folk reputed to have more human attributes as well, and to these we will now turn.

Artist's conception of Cadborosaurus, *the sort of thing described by John Marsh.*

1. Rufus Festus Avienius, *Ora Maritima*, lines 117–29.
2. Carol Rose, *Giants, Monsters, and Dragons: An Encyclopedia of Folklore, Legend, and Myth* (Santa Barbara, CA: ABC-CLIO, 2000), 194.
3. Eric N. Simons, *Into Unknown Waters: John and Sebastian Cabot* (London: Dobson Books, 1964), 175–76.
4. Ingeborg Marshall, *The Beothuk of Newfoundland: A Vanished People* (Vancouver, BC: Douglas & McIntyre, 1977), 33.
5. Charles W. Eliot, ed., "Edward Haies: Sir Humphrey Gilbert's Voyage to Newfoundland," *Voyages and Travels: Ancient and Modern* (New York: P. F. Collier & Son, 1909–1914), 70.
6. John Josselyn as quoted in Richard M. Dorson, *America Begins* (New York: Pantheon, 1950), 28–29.
7. Horace Beck, *Folklore and the Sea* (Brattleboro, VT: Stephen Greene Press, 1973), 255–59.
8. "Trail of the Sea Serpent," *The Atlantic Monthly*, Vol. LIII (1884), 802.
9. Constantine S. Rafinesque, Esquire, "Dissertation on Water Snakes, Sea Snakes, and Sea Serpents," *The American Monthly Magazine and Critical Review*, Vol. I, no. 6 (October 1817), 484.
10. Ibid.
11. David Crantz, *The History of Greenland* (London: Longman, Hurst, Rees, Orme, & Brown, 1820), 310.
12. Hans Rollmann, *The Telegram* (St. John's, NL), October 10, 2009.

13. John Terriak, "Big Eyed Creature," *Them Days*, 12, no. 1 (September 1986), 35.

14. "The Sea Serpent Again," *The Harbour Grace Standard and Conception Bay Advertiser*, September 2, 1878.

15. "The Sea-serpent Shows Himself," *The New York Times*, November 11, 1879.

16. "The Sea Serpent," *The Daily Mail and Empire* (Toronto, ON), August 3, 1895, 10.

17. "Monster of the Deep," *The Evening Telegram* (St. John's, NL), August 25, 1888, A4.

18. "Strange Sighting, The Sea Serpent Again," *The New York Times*, February 5, 1887, 5.

19. Edward R. Snow, *Strange Tales from Nova Scotia to Cape Hatteras* (New York: Cornwall Press, 1949), 43–52.

20. Anonymous, "Giant Leptocephalus," *Nature* (April 2, 1971), 278–79.

21. J. P. O'Neill, *The Great New England Sea Serpent: An Account of Unknown Creatures Sighted* (Rockport, ME: Down East Books, 1999), 168.

22. Mike Dash, "Baron Von Forstner and the U-28 sea serpent of July 1915," *Charles Fort Institute* (December 11, 2009), http://blogs. forteana.org/trackback/93

23. Ibid.

24. Harold T. Wilkins, "Strange Mysteries of the Great War (1935)," *UFO Roundup*, 4, no. 18 (August 25, 1999).

25. "Sea Monsters' Attack Newfoundland Boats," *The New York Times*, September 19, 1922.

26. "Fishermen Fear Sea Monsters," *The Evening Telegram* (St. John's, NL), September 16, 1922.

27. O'Neill, *The Great New England Sea Serpent*, 194–96.

28. "Sea Serpent or Squid?" *The Boston Evening Transcript* (August 28, 1936), 1.

29. Otto Kelland, *Strange and Curious* (St. John's, NL: Creative Publishers, 1997), 36–38.

30. George Budgell, "Labrador Sea Monster," *Them Days*, 26, no. 4 (Summer 1980), 20–21.

31. Jack Fitzgerald, *Newfoundland Adventures* (St. John's, NL: Creative Publishers, 2006), 64–65.

32. Nathan Budgell, *A Newfoundland Son* (Bloomington, IN: AuthorHouse, 2001), 52.

33. J. R. Smallwood, "Dictionary of Newfoundland Dates," *Book of Newfoundland*, Vol. 4 (St. John's, NL: Newfoundland Book Publishers Ltd., 1967), 561.

34. John Ridgway & Chay Blythe, *A Fighting Chance* (Philadelphia, PA: Lippincott Publishing, 1967), 12, 131–32.

35. Jim Wellman, *Final Voyages*, Vol. 1 (St. John's, NL: Flanker Press Ltd., 2003), 54–60.

36. *The Telegram* (St. John's, NL), May 6,1997; "Newfoundland Highlights," *Newfoundland Quarterly* (April 1 to August 15, 2000), 31.

37. *The Telegram* (St. John's, NL), May 6, 1997; Jeff Ducharme, *The Independent* (St. John's, NL), April 10, 2005.

38. Glen Whiffen, *The Telegram* (St. John's, NL), April 6, 2000.

39. "A Strange Sea Creature was Seen Off Cape," *The Globe and Mail* (Toronto, ON), April 10, 2000.

40. Benjamin Radford, "Ogopogo the Chameleon," *Skeptical Inquirer*, 30, no. 1 (January/February 2006), 41–46.

41. Ryan Cleary, "'Monster' Beached," *The Telegram* (St. John's, NL), August 8, 2001.

42. "Another 'Sea Creature': Mysterious Headless Marine Animal Washes Ashore," *The Western Star* (Corner Brook, NL), February 20, 2010, A1.

43. Alisha Morrissey, "Newfoundland Fishermen Snag Sea Monster in Nets," *The Telegram* (St. John's, NL), March 3, 2010.

44. Ibid.

chapter
three

SEA-FOL*k* AND
THEIR FRIENDS

FEW LEGENDARY CREATURES HAVE been around longer or have been more widespread than mer-creatures; that is, mermaids, mermen, selkies, and other sea-dwellers of this strain. They are among the most intriguing of cryptids. The legends about them are amazingly similar worldwide and go back to the beginning of human history.

ATARGATIS, THE SYRIAN GODDESS of fertility and ruler of the seas (also known as the "fish goddess"), was represented as a sort of mermaid as were the *Apsaras* and the *Jalpari* (or water faries) in the Punjab district of what is now India. Several of the tales in *One Thousand and One Arabian Nights* feature sea-people who, unlike their portrayal in other mythologies, were anatomically indistinguishable from humans but for their ability to live under water. In the first century they were considered so factual that Roman historian Pliny the Elder included mermaids in his *Natural History*. Much later

Atargatis, ruler of the seas, here depicted by someone perhaps unclear on the concept of mermaids.

Cynewulf, an English poet who lived between 750 and 1,000 ce, wrote *The Nature of the Siren*:

> Strange things indeed are seen in the sea world;
> Men say that mermaids are like to maidens
> In breast and body. But not so below:
> From the navel netherward nothing looks human
> For they are fishes, and furnished with finds [sic].
> These prodigies dwell in a perilous passage
> Where swirling waters swallow men's vessels...[1]

According to the *Polar Record* of the Scott Polar Research Institute, Cambridge, England, an international scholarly periodical publishing results from a wide range of research areas, the medieval *Konungs Skuggsjá* (*King's Mirror*) describes Iceland and Greenland with remarkable scientific accuracy.[2] A 13th-century instructional guide, believed to be intended for the sons of Norway's Håkon IV Håkonsson, it contains some unusual information. Here there are descriptions of a number of North Atlantic marine creatures, some real and some, no doubt, imagined. A portion of the Konungs Skuggsjá put forward a few years ago by Dr. Ian Whitaker, Department of Sociology and Anthropology, Simon Fraser University, reads:

> The monster called *hafstrambr* [merman] is found in the seas of Greenland. This monster is tall and of great size and rises straight out of the water. It appears to have shoulders, neck and head, eyes and mouth, and nose and chin like those of a human being; but above the eyes and eyebrows it looks more like a man with a peaked helmet on his head [a sea bishop?]. It has shoulders like a man's but no hands. Its body apparently grows narrower from the shoulders down...The form of this prodigy...looked much like an icicle...Whenever this monster has shown itself, men have always been sure that a storm would follow. They have also noted how it has turned when about to plunge into the waves and in what direction it has fallen; if it has turned toward the ship and plunged in that direction, the sailors have felt sure that lives would be lost on that ship; but whenever it has turned away from the vessel and has plunged in that direction, they have felt confident that their lives would be spared, even though they should encounter rough waters and severe storms.

Further along, the natural history lesson continued:

> Another prodigy called *margýgr* [mermaid] has also been

seen there. This appears to have the form of a woman from the waist upward, for it has large nipples on its breast like a woman, long hands and heavy hair, and its neck and head are formed in every respect like a human...Below the waist line it has the shape of a fish with scales and tail and fins...it rearely appears except before violent storms. Its behaviour is often somewhat like this: it will plunge into the waves and will always reappear with fish in its hands; if it then turnes toward the ship, the men have fears they will suffer a great loss of life...[3]

Fig: 3.

Vir marinus
episcopi specie
An 1531 captus
in mari Baltico.

With their reputable men of science producing works such as this, there is little wonder the common people believed in mermaids and such. In more recent years, four possible explanations have been presented to account for the origin of these phenomena.

First – such creatures do not exist and those who claim to have seen them are either liars or unbalanced. This hardly agrees with reality, as many respectable and reliable people have reported encountering them. Baltazar Coyett, Governor of the Islands of the Province of Amboine and President of the Commissioners in Batavia, and Adrien van der Stell, Governor Regent of the Province of Amboine (today, parts of Indonesia) told of a colourful mermaid or sea-wife in 1717:

> SEE-WYF. A monster resembling a Siren, caught near the island of Borne, or Boeren, in the Department of Amboine. It was 59 inches long [145 centimetres], and in proportion as an eel. It lived on land, in a vat full of water, during four days seven hours. From time to time it uttered little cries like those of a mouse. It would not eat, though it was offered small fish, shells, crabs, lobsters, &c...hair, the hue of kelp...webbed olive between the fingers, which each four joints; the fringe round the waist orange with a blue border; the fins green, face slate-grey; delicate row of pink hairs...[4]

Second – witnesses saw a manatee and, since these are rare, perhaps having been long at sea mistook it for the temptress of legend. It is difficult to imagine anyone being at sea *that* long; as well, many reports of mermaids come from latitudes where the water is far too cold for manatees.

A merman caught in the Baltic Sea in 1531, according to 17th-century German author Canon Johann Zahn. It greatly resembles the so-called "sea bishop."

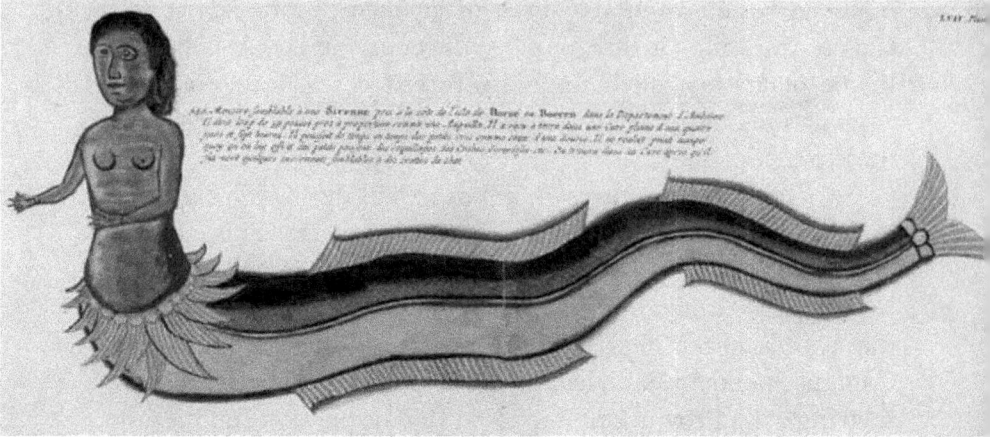

Coyett's sea-wyf.

Third – witnesses actually saw seals. While this might explain an offhand sighting at some distance, it fails to deal with reports of close contact. Most seafarers, particularly those who cruised Newfoundland waters, knew quite well what seals looked like.

Fourth – witnesses saw walruses.[5] This explanation seems even less likely than mistaking a seal for a mermaid. However, in the 1600s the term for walrus was "morse," which may have derived from the Russian *morskoi*, "sea-man." Ultimately "merman" was substituted.[6] Although primarily an Arctic dweller that seldom makes an appearance farther south, the walrus remains a suspect when we check some of the descriptions given of mermen.

Unlike mermaids, mermen are scarcely ever celebrated for their beauty: a number of accounts depict them as bearded with deep-set eyes and covered with reddish hair. Further, they had webbed fingers, and their dental equipment was said to have been quite impressive, with some of them having two large projecting teeth or tusks.[7] Mermen also came in various sizes, from the "bigness of a monkey" to a length of five or six metres, according to the prolific mid-nineteenth-century historian and author Dr. Angelo S. Rappoport.

The descriptions could indeed fit a walrus, and these animals would have been sufficiently rare in European or American waters to be unidentifiable to the average seaman of the day. Stories about mer-people may grow out of man's encounter with the rare or abnormal; it would be a very human response to describe what is unknown or mysterious in terms of existing knowledge and beliefs. Hence, it is possible that any or all of these creatures could have been responsible for such numerous and varied sightings.[8]

МОРСКІЯ СИРЕНЫ.

Morskiy, Siryoni, *or a morse and a siren.*

Mermaids, thought to be nearly human, usually had long hair, breasts, and a tail resembling that of a cod. Often, but not always, they were said to be blue-eyed beauties with golden hair à la Daryl Hannah. Commonly seen sitting on tidal rocks, ledges, or reefs, sometimes wearing a cap, shawl, or veil, mermaids spent much of their time combing their long tresses while gazing into their mirrors and singing.

On rare occcasions, they were said to come ashore in the guise of mortals, and during the Middle Ages the mermaid was considered an agent of the Devil and a symbol of deceit. Most believed they were destructive to humans, either luring unwary seafarers onto reefs with their beauty and captivating voices or presaging storm and destruction simply by being seen, as described in the *Konungs Skuggsjá*.

This idea of calamity following sightings of these seafolk was so widespread and ingrained that an old ballad, "The Mermaid," dating back at least to the mid-1700s begins:

> Last Friday morn when we set sail,
> We hadn't sailed far from land,
> Till we spied, till we spied,
> A pretty fair maid,
> With a comb and glass in her hand,
> Her hand, her hand,
> With a comb and a glass in her hand.

This image prepares us for the disaster that will certainly follow:

> The moon shines bright, the stars give light,
> And my mother is looking for me;
> She may look, she may look with a watery eye,
> She may look to the bottom of the sea,
> The sea, the sea,
> She may look to the bottom of the sea.[9]

The idealized mermaid of more recent times.

A woodcut from the 1700s depicting a traditional mermaid, according to the viewer's description and the artist's ability.

Though ordinarily thought by seafarers to foreshadow peril and death, the mermaid occasionally showed a more benevolent side. Regional tales from the British Isles say that when rescued from danger, mermaids have given humans knowledge of cures for otherwise fatal sicknesses, rich gifts and, again, warnings of storms. Though they may sometimes consort with humans – the offspring of such unions are said to have webbed feet and fingers – they usually return to their watery world and their true partners, the mermen. With a reputation for more frightful conduct, mermen were thought to be aggressive toward mermaids and on occasion devoured their own young.[10]

These sea-folk, part of centuries-old seagoing cultures, were considered to be as real and as common as herring. It would be many years before anyone thought differently, as explorers, adventurers, and the clergy were prominent among those encountering the creatures.

Christopher Columbus, doubtless following the navigational advice of a predecessor, had slowly made his way westward across the Atlantic on the famous voyage that he had begun on August 3, 1492. On January 9, 1493, when in the vicinity of Hispaniola, the astute captain made the following entry in *Santa Maria*'s log:

> In a bight at the coast of Hispaniola, I saw three sirens... they came very high out of the water...but they are not so beautiful as they are painted, though to some extent they have a human appearance about the face.

A merman of the monster variety, just one of naturalist Ulisse Aldrovandi's grotesque creatures.

Could this, the somewhat unlovely manatee, have been Columbus's mermaid?

83

Further, he said he had seen others previously in Guinea, on the coast of Manigueta (today's Liberia and Sierra Leone), and they were no more attractive.[11] Today many argue, in particular William S. Stevens in *Five Hundred Magazine*, that Columbus had seen manatees; this may well have been the case as these beasts inhabit the coasts of the Caribbean, the Amazon region, and West Africa.[12]

A different matter altogether was a report dated November 3, 1523, from Ambroise Paré who would go on to become the French Surgeon General. He had apparently seen and examined somewhat closely a merman the size of a five-year-old human that was "like to a man even to the navell [sic], except the ears; in the other parts it resembled a fish."[13] Of course this may have been another case of mistaken identity, but the man did become chief surgeon to both Charles IX and Henri III. He was also considered a true Renaissance man and, arguably, the outstanding physician of the 16th century. His book *Des Monstres et prodiges* (*On Monsters and Marvels*), suggests that he certainly believed such things existed.

Naturalist and author Richard Carrington confirmed that in the 1600s mer-folk were commonplace and their existence was as firmly established as the existence of shrimps.[14] They were supposedly seen off the European coast, and travellers brought back tales of encounters with them from every corner of the world.

In 1608, Hendrik (Henry) Hudson, another reputable attestant, said that the crew of his ship, *Hopewell*, had reported seeing a mermaid. We can be quite certain this one was not a manatee, since the sighting was at 75 degrees, not far south of Iceland's latitude. Hudson recorded the event of June 15 in his journal:

> This morning one of our companie looking over boord saw
> a Mermaid...from Navill upward, her back and breasts were
> like a woman's (as they say that saw her) her body as big

as one of us; her skin very white; and long haire hanging down behinde, of color blacke; in her going downe they saw her tayle, which was like the tayle of a porposse and speckled like a Macrell.

The chief witnesses were Thomas Hilles and Robert Rayner, and judging by Hudson's phlegmatic entry in the log, he obviously believed in mermaids as well.[15] It could also be that good ol' Tom and Bob were having a bit of fun at the skipper's expense.

Two years later, Newfoundland's most famous mer-creature was reported by explorer and entrepreneur Captain Sir Richard Whitbourne. This saltwater stunner appeared in St. John's Harbour near the mouth of the Waterford River. It was a fine June day in 1610 when the unexpected caller both frightened and astonished onlookers along the shore and in their boats. Whitbourne, who witnessed the surprising sequence of events, had a good look at the creature and for a brief period was certain it was going to attack him. He entered the exciting experience in his diary:

Now also I will not omit to relate something of a strange Creature that I first saw there in the yeere 1610. In a morn-ing early as I was standing by the water side, in the Harbour of Saint Johns, which I espied verie swiftly to come swimming towards me, looking cheerefully, as it had beene a woman, by the Face, Eyes, Nose, Mouth, Chin eares, Necke and Forehead: It seemed to be so beautifull, and in those parts so well proportioned, having round about upon the head, all blew strakes, resembling haire, downe to the Necke (but certainly it was haire) for I beheld it long, and another of my companie also, yet living, that was not then farre from me; and seeing the same comming so swiftly towards mee, I stepped backe, for it was come within the length of a long Pike. Which when this strange Creature saw that I went from it, it presently thereupon dived a little under water, and did swim to the place where before I landed whereby I beheld the shoulders and backe downe to the middle, to be as square, white and smooth as the backe of a man, and from the middle to the hinder part, pointing in proportion like a broad hooked Arrow; how it was proportioned in the forepart from the necke and shoulders, I know not; but the same came shortly after unto a Boat, wherein one William Hawkridge, then my servant, was, that hath bin since a Captaine in a Ship to the East Indies, and is lately there imploied againe by Sir Thomas Smith, in the like Voyage; and the same Creature did put both his hands upon the side of the Boate, and did strive to come in to him and others then in the said Boate: whereat they were afraid; and one of them strooke it a full blow on the head; whereat it fell off from them: and afterwards it came to two other Boates in the Harbour; the men in them, for feare fled to land: This (I suppose) was a Mermaide. Now because divers have written much of Mermaides, I have presumed to relate, what is most certaine of such a strange Creature that was scene at New-found-land: whether it were a Mermaide or no, I know not; I leave it for others to judge, &c. R. W.[16]

Some propose that it had been a seal, but certainly a master mariner and ex-fisherman such as Whitbourne would have known a seal when he saw one. Beyond question, he was genuinely mystified.

Later that evening, two men were pushing their boat, loaded with firewood, away from a beach on the south side of the harbour when a strange creature – presumably the same one, it being a woman from the waist up – placed its hands on the gunwales and seemed to be pleading with them. Terrified, the two left their boat to the mermaid and dashed madly off into the woods.[17] Some time later they emerged, found the creature gone, and returned home to explain to their wives why they

Richard Whitbourne evidently chatting with a mermaid in St. John's.

were so late, where they had been, and what they had been up to. We have had no news of them since.

Captain John Smith, perhaps best known for his presumed dalliance with Pocahontas, mentioned seeing mermaids in 1614. He, too, had commendable clarity of vision and mind, as he also commented that they were not as beautiful as artists had depicted them. He described her as swimming "with grace," having large eyes, finely shaped nose that was "somewhat short," and "well-formed ears that were rather too long." Also her "long green hair imparted to her an original character by no means unattractive." He frankly admitted that he had begun to experience "the first effect of love" until he realized that from the waist down, she was a fish.[18]

Johann Ludwig Gottfried mentioned a Captain Hailbourne in his *Newe Welt vnd americanische Historien* (Frankfurt, 1655) who visited St. John's. This worthy, too, had an encounter with mermaids as he approached the Newfoundland coast. He not only saw them, he was quite certain they beckoned to him. However, his description was sufficiently vague to cast doubt on the creature's identity; his report could have been, at worst, a complete fabrication or, at best, wishful thinking. The creatures were never accurately identified, and we have no other record of this sighting. Likewise, no other information has been found regarding Hailbourne; it may well have been that Gottfried confused it with Whitbourne's experience or a similar event, as others have done.

In 1660, Francisco de la Vega Caz, the Spanish merman or *hombre pez*, was born in Liérganes, Spain. In 1674, he took to the sea, and it was not until five years later that he was caught in fishing nets near Cadiz. Upon being hauled out, Señor Caz cried out, "*Pan, vino, tobacco,*" – bread, wine, tobacco. Upon hearing this, the sailors realized he was a Christian and a countryman and soon discovered that his home had been Liérganes, a municipality located in the autonomous community of Cantabria in northern Spain and some kilometres inland.

Francisco, who had short red hair, vacant eyes, colourless flabby flesh, some scales, and a pronounced aversion to clothing, was returned to his home town. Left with his family, he refused to speak further and eventually, like a fish out of water, sickened of life on land and returned to the sea to disappear again among his finny friends. The history of the amphibious adventurer was vouched for by Spanish archbishops, and even Feijóo, the refuter of popular fallacies, gave the whole account his blessing.[19]

Benoît de Maillet, in his *Téliamède*, gave an account of a mermaid seen by the crew of a French ship off the coast of Newfoundland in 1725. They observed it for some hours, and the captain considered it important enough to warrant sending a report back to France. All who could write signed a statement which was forwarded to their Minister of Marine, Jean-Frédéric Phélypeaux, comte de Maurepas.[20]

As late as 1755 someone identified only as "P. C." submitted an article addressed to Mr. Urban of *The Gentleman's Magazine and Historical Chronicle* of London. The writer indicated that he was, even then, not sure that Whitbourne's report should be treated lightly:

> There are still many people who doubt the existence of the Mermaid, and perhaps with good reason, yet all natural historians deliver as a fact, and the many relations of navigators of credit should not be wholly disregarded. I beg leave to give you a relation that I lately met with in a very scarce pamphlet, intitled, A Discourse and Discovery of Newfoundland by Capt. Rd. Whitbourne. London, 1622. I am Yours & c. P.C.[21]

The legendary sea-folk were still being taken quite seriously, and a great debate arose among learned men early in that century when they heard reports that natives of Angola were catching mermaids and eating them as a matter of course. The problem these scholars and clergymen faced was not whether mermaids existed, but whether this was cannibalism and how best to punish the perpetrators if, indeed, it was happening. Not unexpectedly, after much deliberation and rhetoric, they reached no conclusion.[22]

But it was not just European explorers who chanced upon members of these seagoing tribes. Not surprisingly, they were said to exist here long before the arrival of adventurers from across the Atlantic. In folklore of the Labrador Innu, one finds a sea monster known as *Auvekoejak*, similar to mer-people but covered with fur rather than scales, which gulped down whole shoals of fish in its perpetual hunger. In the mid-1700s, despite calling the fur seal by the same name, the Innu still insisted that the *Auvekoejak* and the seal were two distinct entities. Their insistence casts great doubt on the possibility of the *Auvekoejak* being either the familiar seal or walrus of the region – exactly what they were referring to may never be known.[23]

Canada, too, had its problems with mer-people. In Montreal, on November 13, 1812, Venant St. Germain appeared before the Court of King's Bench and swore an affidavit that he had seen a mermaid on Lake Superior. A respected citizen of Lower Canada, St. Germain was Seigneur of Repentigny and a fur trader with the North West Company. Two judges of the court heard the declaration and attested to it having been "sworn before us."[24]

Great credence was still being given to reports of mer-folk in the 1800s, so much so that some Japanese made good money selling stuffed mermaids to gullible European adventurers, who would be better known as tourists today. These fabulous creatures were fashioned by sewing the upper torso of a monkey to the tail end of a fish and more or less mummifying the result so it resembled a sort of deformed and repulsive sushi.

There was one mermaid – more correctly a merman – that was a particularly outlandish hoax. In England, a crackpot named Robert Hawks frequently disguised himself as a mermaid, sat on a rock, and sang in the moonlight – much to the awe and consternation of local villagers. Bad luck for him, appreciation of this type of humour was rapidly disappearing, and he was forced to find a vocation for which he was better suited. Some years later he found his niche and donned the holy robes of the ministry.[25] And,

P. T. Barnum's Feejee mermaid.

speaking of hoaxes, we must not forget P. T. Barnum's grotesque and famous Feejee mermaid of 1842, which, too, was made in Japan by the traditional method.

Here at home in the mid-1800s, a singular story emerged when an American diver, who was working on a wreck at St. Shott's Rock, found his tasks nearly beyond his capabilities because of strong currents and undertow. On the verge of giving up, he was surprised when a stranger appeared beside him, took the ropes he was trying to secure, and completed the job. Startled at first, he then wondered who it was and where he had come from. In the murky water, it was difficult to be certain of the identity of anyone or anything.

His helper stayed around, and the diver, having regained his composure, continued his work. Gradually, he discerned that his helper had the body of a woman from the waist up, but from the centre of the back and down, the torso tapered to a large tail. The shocked diver stated emphatically that he could never have carried out the salvage work without his aquatic benefactor.[26]

Could this have been a case of narcosis, an effect on the brain of divers brought about by gaseous nitrogen? Among the symptoms are impaired judgment, confusion, and hallucinations. Perhaps P. J. Wakeham, one of Newfoundland's premier story-tellers of the mid-twentieth century, concocted the entire event. Or could it be that there really was a mermaid?

Otto Kelland, respected author and all-round Newfound-land icon, related a story told by his grandmother of the strange experience of a shore fisherman near Grand Bank in the 1890s. Men, standing on the prominence overlooking the harbour entrance, saw a dory being rowed toward them at a phenomenal speed. The men could see nothing that would give such impetus to the rower, but they easily perceived that something was wrong.

Rushing to the beach, they arrived in time to see the worn-out oarsman, Sam Green, leap from his boat, lapse into

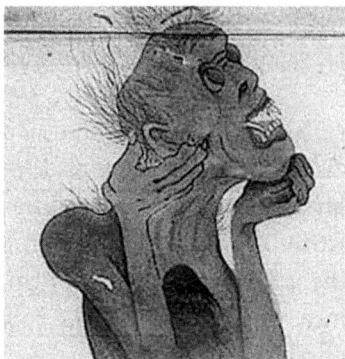

*What did Sam Green see?
Was it as horrible as this Japanese
sea-person?*

unconsciousness, and crumple to the ground. They fetched the doctor who, after reviving poor Sam, had him taken home where he sedated him. Next morning, the doctor stopped by and asked the recovering man about the events leading up to his arrival on the beach in such desperate condition. Green explained that while fishing he had hooked what he assumed to be an enormous cod: As he hauled his line in, his catch had put up quite a struggle. Just when he expected to see his fine fish break the surface, he was confronted by a grotesque humanoid – at least that portion above water seemed to be so. The body was covered with short grey hair, its eyes, nose, and mouth set on a round head were much like those of a monkey; its ears were quite large, its hands webbed.

Apparently, what really traumatized the fisherman was the unintelligible speech issuing from the creature's torn mouth while it frantically pointed, indicating that it wanted the hook removed. With the line cut, the creature vanished into the depths.[27] The terrified fisherman soon found a less nerve-wracking job.

A well-known Rushoon fisherman and schooner-builder of the early 1900s, Skipper Joe Cheeseman, had a race with something he identified as Satan. The description of this entity is a rather odd one, though it fits that of a typical merman if such can be termed typical.

Cheeseman had taken some friends in his skiff from Rushoon, on the west side of Placentia Bay, to St. Joseph's, about ten kilometres up the shore, for a Saturday night dance. After the dance had broken up, sometime past midnight, the still festive revellers boarded the boat and set out for home.

The light craft fairly flew across the still water and one of the boisterous rowers chortled, "The Devil himself couldn't catch us tonight!" The young men rocked with laughter, but then they saw a shape in the water behind them that stifled their levity. The strange form rapidly gained on them until it materialized into what appeared to be the head and shoulders of a man, yet it did not seem to be swimming. They were mystified as to its means of propulsion.

The men, by now apprehensive, kept rowing at speed, but the creature gained rapidly. Despite their best efforts, it continued to close the distance, and they very nearly had a collective stroke when it caught up to them and clambered into the boat. Manlike, but covered with black hair, it stood there stolidly and ignored the panicked men flailing at it with their oars. They were certain Satan had them, and one terrified man in the bow cried, "For God's sake, return to where you came from!" The hairy shape promptly dropped back over the gunwale, and sank. Joe Cheeseman and those with him solemnly swore that this event occurred exactly as they described it, and it soon became legend.[28]

Mer-people continued to plague our coasts, and around the beginning of the 20th century Alfred Gatehouse (1870–1941) of Change Islands reported having seen a mermaid with long hair streaming down her shoulders. As far as residents were concerned it could be nothing less than a mermaid if Alf Gatehouse said so, but Canon George Earle wondered if it may have been a rare horsehead seal. Still, Mr. Gatehouse was familiar with both horses and seals of all types, and that seal's distinctive horse-head should have tipped him off to the fact that it was not one of our even rarer marine lovelies.[29]

According to some old-timers – among them, again, P. J. Wakeham – another case of a potential and unwanted passenger took place in the St. John's Narrows in 1912, when a strange marine creature attempted to climb into a dory. The men in the boat said it was much like a beautiful woman but had blue streaks on its head formed by a hairlike growth. It was about 4.5 metres long, including its fishlike tail, and that is a pretty big mermaid (about the same size as Whitbourne's). No verifying accounts have been found in newspapers of the day, but that means little. However, the description is so similar to that given by Whitbourne that we must suspect at once that Wakeham had simply updated that old account. [30]

Under what conditions would an old fisherman such as Alf Gatehouse mistake a horsehead or grey seal for a mermaid?

The disconcerting experience of a pair of unnamed hunters at Cat Arm, White Bay, in 1915 was very unlike other reports. Typical of many hunters today, upon seeing something in the water, one of them shot at it without knowing what it was. The target sank from sight, and they marked the point of its disappearance, certain it had been hit. It took but a short time for them to find their victim; they were stunned to find that a dead merman, with black hair and a beard, had washed ashore.[31] What became of the unusual bag was not recorded.

Others of these extraordinary beings were apparently well-meaning, as was the diver's helper at St. Shott's. On one occasion a man in a small boat, caught in a heavy gale, was in danger of being driven onto the rocks. Just when he had resigned himself to making the acquaintance of Davey Jones, one of these mermen appeared, scrambled into his boat, and conned it through the breakers to the safety of the beach beyond.[32] Would that we had more of these helpful individuals.

Mer-creatures were quite plentiful around that time. A south coast fisherman, hand-lining from his dory just off shore, had stopped at midday to eat his lunch. While taking it from his breadbox, he heard something and turned to find a merman attempting to climb into his boat. Flabbergasted by the impudence of his uninvited guest, he tried, without success, to scare him off by shouting. Finally, losing patience, he gave the creature a good whack on the fingers with his gaff; this apparently caused him to lose his appetite and go on his way.[33] No description of this particular freeloader has been found, but in more recent years creatures similar to those which approached the fishermen of Cat Arm and those on the south coast were reported in northwest Bonavista Bay.

Some say that the bigfoot of Newfoundland have a preference for living on or about the cliffs along shore; perhaps the following should be included in the chapter on that particular beast because, as we shall see, there are startling similarities.[34]

The creature Charlie and David Blackwood saw seemed to move between land and sea with considerable ease. In August 1971, the two cousins, 25 and 33 years of age respectively, took their boat out of Brookfield to hunt birds around the many islands of the area. They were totally unprepared for what they found.

Around 3:00 p.m. a thick fog rolled in and caught them out past Cabot Islands, about 15 kilometres directly east of Pound Cove. They decided to head home and spent a half-hour fumbling about in the murk passing, again, what they were certain were the Cabot Islands – then their motor coughed and sputtered to a halt.

It took an hour to restart it by dint of mechanical aptitude and coarse language, but by then wind and tide had carried them a significant distance. Now they had no idea where they were, but finally, through a rift in the fog, Charlie spied land that he believed to be Stevensons Islets.

As they neared a small beach, movement caught their attention. Atop the cliff which ran the length of the islet stood two peculiar entities. Abruptly, the men's progress slowed, and their way fell off. The creatures were little more than 125 centimetres tall, had very short arms and legs, prominent ears, no perceptible neck, and were covered with grey fur. At that distance there was no clear evidence of eyes or nose. The strange beings watched the men silently, then casually descended the near vertical cliff and slipped into the sea.

Now, disinclined to land, the Blackwoods stood offshore that night and did not dare sleep. At dawn the fog lifted, and they returned home to tell of their chilling brush with the unknown.[35] There have been no further reports of these beings, so perhaps they were merely visitors.

Are there really mermaids and mermen? If so, are we related? In defiance of most mainstream scientists, Elaine Morgan has made a noteworthy attempt in her seminal book, *The Aquatic Ape,* to explain why humans have adaptations not found in other land-bound mammals. Our general lack of hair has been blamed on the intense heat of the savannah, but Morgan insists that if this were the case, other hunters such as the hyena, lion, and cheetah, would also be hairless. She holds that humans returned to the sea, much as whales and other cetaceans are believed to have done. However, she postulates that humans re-emerged from the ocean to live on land once again, and after this aquatic evolutionary detour, they were naked when compared to other apes.

Morgan contends that we lost our hair for the same reason whales and dolphins lost theirs. Her thinking is that any fairly large marine mammal needing to keep warm in the water would be better served by a layer of fat on the inside of its skin than by a layer of hair on the outside. She also points out that while humans are the only weeping primates, seals and other sea mammals shed tears. Many have argued strenuously against her theory and assure us that it is ludicrous in the extreme. However, Morgan has at least caused some self-styled experts to put on their thinking caps for a change. Perhaps our presumed mythical aquatic friends *are* those relatives who took this different path and, rather than return to land, remained with their ancestral allies.[36]

1. Simon Winchester, *Atlantic* (New York: Harper Collins, 2010), 158.
2. Waldemar H. Lehn & Irmgard I. Schroeder, "*Hafgerdingar*: A Mystery from the King's Mirror Explained," *Polar Record* 39, issue 03 (2003), 211–17.
3. I. Whitaker, "North Atlantic Sea Creatures in the King's Mirror (*Konungs Skuggsjá*)," *Polar Record*, 23, issue 142 (1986), 6–7.
   All errors appear in original.

4. Lionel & Patricia Fanthorpe, *Unsolved Mysteries of the Sea* (Toronto, ON: Dundurn Press, 2004), 35–36.

5. Dr. Angelo S. Rappoport, *Superstitions of Sailors* (London: S. Paul & Co. Ltd., 1928), 190.

6. Ibid.

7. Sabine Baring-Gould, *Curious Myths of the Middle Ages* (London: Gilbert & Rivington Printers, 1876), 230–58.

8. John Josselyn, *An Account of Two Voyages to New-England* (London: printed for Giles Widdows, 1674), 228.

9. Gwen Benwell & Arthur Waugh, *Sea Enchantress: The Tale of the Mermaid and Her Kin* (London: Hutchinson, 1961), 243.

10. Carol Rose, *Giants, Monsters, and Dragons: An Encyclopedia of Folklore, Legend, and Myth* (Santa Barbara, CA: ABC-CLIO, 2000), 243–44.

11. J. Franklin Jameson, ed., "The Northmen, Columbus, and Cabot, 985–1503," *Original Narratives of Early American History* (New York: Charles Scribner & Sons, 1906), 218.

12. William S. Stevens, *Five Hundred Magazine*, 1, no. 1 (May/June 1989).

13. Ambroise Paré, *Des Monstres et prodiges*, (1573), translated by Janis L. Pallister (London: University of Chicago Press, 1982), 107.

14. Richard Carrington, *Mermaids and Mastodons: A Book of Natural and Unnatural History* (New York: Rinehart & Company, 1957), 139.

15. Donald P. Wharton, "Hudson's Mermaid: Symbol and Myth in Early American Sea Literature," *Early American Literature and Culture: Essays Honoring Harrison T. Meserole*, edited by Kathryn Zabelle Derounian-Stodola (Cranbury, NJ: Associated University Press, 1992), 38–39.

16. Richard Whitbourne, *A Discourse and Discovery of Newfoundland* (London: Felix Kyngston, for William Barret, 1620), Conclusion 3–4.

17. "A Brief History of Navigation," *The Saturday Magazine*, no. 417, Supplement (December 1838), 255.

18. Jerome Clark, *Unexplained* (Farmington Mills, MI: Visible Ink Press, 1999), 462.

19. Richard Ford, FSA, *A Handbook for Travellers in Spain*, Part II (London: John Murray, 1855), 869–70.

20. "Old and New Mermaids, and the Superstition Connected with the Belief in Mermaids," *The Asiatic Journal and Monthly Register for British India and its Dependencies*, Vol. XV (January to June, 1823), 50.

21. P. C., "Curious Account of a Merman, or Mermaid," *The Gentleman's Magazine and Historical Chronicle*, Vol. XXV (1755), 504.

22. Peter Freuchen, *Peter Freuchen's Book of the Seven Seas* (New York: Julian Messner Inc., 1957), 483.

23. Rose, *Giants, Monsters, and Dragons*, 32; see also Kenneth McLeish, *Myths and Legends of the World Explored* (London: Bloomsbury Press, 1996).

24. Gordon Johnston, *More It Happened in Canada* (Richmond Hill, ON: Scholastic-TAB Publications, 1976).

25. Benwell & Waugh, *Sea Enchantress*, 121.

26. P. J. Wakeham, *New-Land Magazine* (Autumn-Winter, 1980–1981), 115–19.

27. Otto Kelland, *Strange and Curious* (St. John's, NL: Creative Publishers, 1997), 33–35.

28. Jack Fitzgerald, *Newfoundland's Believe It or Not* (Mount Pearl, NL: Chronicle Publishing, 1974), 31.

29. George H. Earle, *A Collection of Foolishness & Folklore* (St. John's, NL: Harry Cuff Publications, 1988), 56.

30. P. J. Wakeham, *New-Land Magazine*, 115–19.

31. Horace Beck, *Folklore and the Sea* (Brattleboro, VT: Stephen Greene Press, 1973), 249.

32. Benwell & Waugh, *Sea Enchantress*, 145.

33. Beck, *Folklore and the Sea*, 249; Rose, *Giants, Monsters, and Dragons*, 244.

34. Dawn Prince-Hughes, *The Archetype of the Ape-man: The Phenomenological Archaeology of a Relic Hominid Ancestor*, Dissertation.com, U.S.A. (1997), 65.

35. Kelland, *Strange and Curious*, 25–30.

36. Elaine Morgan, *The Aquatic Ape* (New York: Stein & Day Publishers, 1982).

chapter

four

WOODUM HAOOT,
THE POND DeMONS

ONCE, ON PLACENTIA BAY'S Long Island and directly east of
the north end of Barren Haven Island, lay the fishing station
of La Plant, its minuscule harbour suitable only for small
boats. Still, it was used by the French as a seasonal post more
than 200 years ago and later became a tiny semi-settlement
offering winter shelter to livyers from around the bay. One of its
attractions was the substantial forest, which not only broke the
fierce winds but provided house and boat building material and
firewood.

About 700 metres to the southwest of La Plant lay a pond,
not more than 400 metres long by 150 wide. It was here in this
small body of water that, according to a one-time winter
resident, a monster of sorts lived. He described it as a gigantic
lobster, and he had seen it leave a three-metre-wide trail in
the snow as it made its way back to the pond. He contended that
he had watched it vanish down a hole in the ice and conscien-
tiously reported, "You'd 'a thought a big steamer had been

Was it a crustacean such as this man-snatcher that resided in the pond near La Plant?

la'nched, so much water was throwed up."[1] No other witnesses have come forward to confirm or challenge the evidence, so perhaps we should take the account with a grain of salt. But can we be certain it was only his imagination? Numerous such cases crop up in folklore.

The Innu in particular have passed down tales of many places where uncommon creatures may lurk. In fact, they have bestowed names commemorating encounters with strange beasts or beings upon more than a dozen of these locations. One of these toponymic monuments lies some 33 kilometres east-southeast of Lake Melville's Etagaulet Bay, on the eastern side of the Mealy Mountains. This location, with a body of water only eight kilometres long and a mere two-and-a-half across at its widest point, offered a fine campsite for the nomadic people of the area.

One warm and sunny day, a group of Innu children were playing in the shallow waters near their temporary home while their parents tended to the business of survival in that harsh land. The high-spirited youngsters paid little heed to the possibility of danger, but luckily hunters on a hill overlooking the lake spied an immense and unfamiliar beast stealthily approaching them through the calm shoals.

The men cried a warning, and the children, now alerted to the menace, made all haste for the shore, screaming. They had scarcely gained safety when the villainous creature thrashed its way into the shallows, mouth agape. Foiled in its attempt to get an easy meal, the disgruntled monster returned to the waters of its small home and disappeared beneath the surface.

The legend has the brute as black with a spoon-shaped head and a rather nondescript tail, and greatly resembling a gigantic *amishku-utikuma* or beaver beetle (*Leptinillus validus*). This scavenging arachnid prowls the coats of the common North American beaver and is familiar to all who trap that animal. The frightening event has been memorialized by the Innu in the name of that body of water, *Manitupeku* or Evil Creature Lake.[2]

Uenitshikumishiteu (also *Wentshukumishiteu*) is another fearsome water-dwelling spirit or monster of Innu legend. Though it travels mostly beneath the surface or under the ice, this otterlike being can pop up just about anywhere, regardless of the thickness of the ice. The fact that they were also inordinately fond of human flesh has done little to promote their image among the Innu.[3] Besides being able to plough through ice, it can travel underground, and even rock presents no great obstacle. Reputedly, one of its haunts is under *Manitu-utshu* (Spirit Mountain or Monster Mountain), a monolithic knoll towering 120 metres or so above Muskrat Falls on the north side of the Churchill River, where a gravel dyke constricts the water to constitute the raging torrent which features so prominently in today's news.

The rocky headland on the right of Muskrat Falls is Manitu-utshu.

In some tales, *Uenitshikumishiteu*'s actions are benevolent, while in others the creature is a feared and relentless menace to all. Strangely, the Innu all agree that it is fiercely protective of the young of other animals, particularly those of the otter, and zealously defends them from human hunters.[4]

The few existing stories about the creature suggest the events related took place long ago and have probably been revised significantly over the intervening years. In 1994, Etien Rich of Sheshatshiu told of two Innu from Natashquan who were in the area of Muskrat Falls when they spotted a pair of young otter, one of which was white. While one man stayed back, the other crept up on the animals and with a single shot bagged the white pup. At that moment his friend heard growling from the water and a great wave suddenly erupted. The hunter who had killed the pup turned and raced toward his friend, and as the ground trembled and formed ripples in sympathy with the water, the diabolical spirit snatched him up. When it did so the ground opened up, swallowing it and the screaming man.[5]

At the same time Greg Penashue also had a tale to tell. His father had spoken, as did his uncle Edward Rich, of the evil creature that dwelt near Spirit Mountain. At night, in their camp near Mekentsheu-shipiss (the MacKenzie River), they heard the river ice cracking loudly in the distance. Next day they were surprised to find the extremely thick ice had a nearly perfectly round hole in it, as if something had broken through from below. They believed the only creature capable of such a tremendous feat was the malignant being they knew as *Uenitshikumishiteu*.[6]

Matshi-nipi, or Bad Lake, is 190 kilometres north of Happy Valley-Goose Bay, and though it is only around seven kilometres

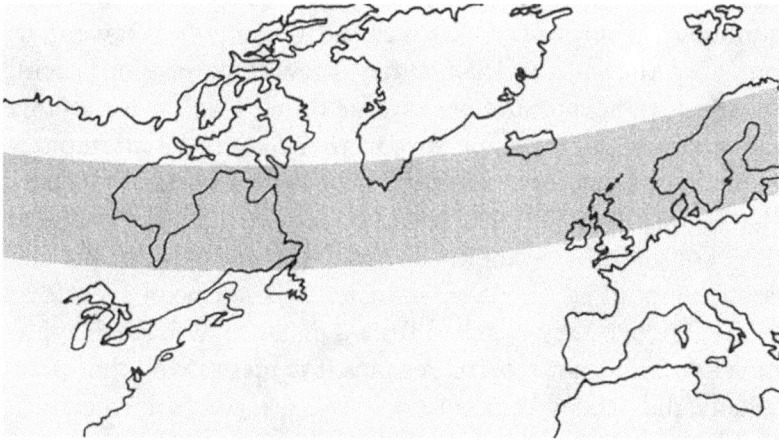

Lake creatures seem to reside in what is called the "Lake monster belt," which extends across northern Europe and North America.

long and five wide, it is quite deep and is said to be inhabited by an enormous and dangerous creature. Many Innu have seen it, and some have said its head resembled that of a chicken while others thought it was more foxlike. But it bothers no one unless provoked.

Stories of lake monsters in Newfoundland and Labrador are not unique to Innu culture, of course. And, like reports of sea monsters and mer-folk, they are often presented by quite unlikely people. Reverend Gordon Elliot was appointed to the Anglican Mission of Whitbourne where he resided from 1924 to 1928. Returning to England in 1936, he was Honorary Chaplain of Canterbury Cathedral from 1944 to 1947, at which time he returned to Newfoundland as Rector of Foxtrap Parish until his retirement.

The reverend reckoned the surroundings of woods and ponds to be delightful, as he dearly loved the outdoors. The only fly in his bucolic ointment was what he called "our own edition of the Loch Ness Monster." Something resided in Rocky Pond, now known as Bethune's Pond, on the Hodge River, south of the town. It just suddenly appeared out of nowhere one summer. What it was, where it came from, or where it went, no one ever knew (or at least if they knew they were not saying so). Residents were sure of only one thing: There was a strange and colossal fish of some sort in their pond. All attempts to identify or capture it were futile, but Reverend Elliott insisted that it was there. "We saw it and it was a living thing!"[7]

For months residents avoided the area; then one day someone pointed out their monster had not been seen for a while. Though they watched from a distance with some apprehension, it did not return. Perhaps it is just as well that it left when it did – today Whitbourne's sewage lagoon drains into the pond.

An odd creature showed up in Gander Lake in the 1930s, and while it was not what we commonly understand to be a lake monster, it certainly was strange. The enigmatic invertebrate, said to resemble a lobster, was between 25 and 35 centimetres long, had fishlike eyes, pincers of seven or eight centimetres in length, and three pairs of legs, but it did not have the segmented tail of the lobster. Locally, it was inelegantly called a "maggot," but possibly this presumed crustacean was related to, or was, the squat lobster (*Munidopsis andamanica*) or *langostino*. The latter is the Spanish diminutive for *langosta*, lobster, and is commonly used to refer to the meat of the squat lobster, which is neither a true lobster nor a prawn but more closely related to hermit crabs. Today it is sold in many restaurants instead of the more expensive beast we know as lobsters (*Homarus americanus*). It is not known how long they remained in the lake, but it seems they eventually departed, as none have been seen in years.

Gander Lake is some 56 kilometres long with a maximum width of seven kilometres and a confirmed depth of at least 275 metres. However, its uncommon lake-bottom geography,

The squat lobster, possibly Gander Lake's "maggot."

currents, and even tides have consistently defied efforts to define its depth, and it is thought to be much deeper. A body of water this size could conceal virtually anything. The lake is considered oligotrophic (i.e., it provides little to sustain life), but the deep-sea squat lobster and its cousins cannot afford to be picky if they want to survive. Of necessity they can feed on a wide range of seemingly inedible substances, and recently it was proven that wood can be one of their primary sources of nutrition. This is the one material that was perhaps plentiful in Gander Lake, the wooded shores of which, since the late 1800s, have hosted a considerable forest industry. The creepy brutes were completely forgotten until 1952 when they were rediscovered at Swanger's Cove, on the west side of Bay d'Espoir. Evidently, it may not be a *bona fide* lake monster after all, but a sort of sea monster.[8] It is not known if they can still be found there.

No one has determined its origin, species, or even its genus, but some uninformed individuals have thought it may have been a misidentification of the common lobster of eastern North America customarily found in Newfoundland waters. That, however, is patently ridiculous as this latter creature is so familiar to Newfoundlanders that such a mistake would be well-nigh impossible. Since there is probably no law against catching lobsters in a true lake, lovers of seafood would have had a field day, and our maggots would have become extinct in no time flat. Once again, no one thought it worthwhile to have the creature identified or have one preserved. Such neglect discourages even fruitful speculation.

Another man of the cloth – and the epitome of moral rectitude – Moravian missionary Reverend Frederick W. Peacock served in Labrador from 1935 until 1971. Peacock was an authority on the area and its people; in fact, he gained a master's degree in social anthropology in 1948 through his study of the natives and their ways. This, perhaps, lends greater credence to his observations regarding these people and their beliefs than would normally be the case.

Peacock told of a large lake on Okak Island (which is in reality *islands*) said to be home to a tremendous water monster. Since the largest body of water on the islands is more of a pond on the northwest end of the northernmost island, about two kilometres long and a kilometre wide, the large lake Peacock referred to may well have been the 15-kilometre-long tickle between the north and south islands.

The monster was said by natives to have a very large head and the body of a seal, which led some outsiders to think it was likely a bearded seal. However, this is hardly plausible as that creature is medium-sized, a bit more than two metres nose-to-tail length, and weighs in at only 275 to 350 kilograms. The Innu have used its skin since time immemorial to cover their larger boats, so it is unlikely they would not have recognized their old friend.[9]

In the 1990s, artist Bill Ritchie of Nain said that Edward Noah had told him the Innu believe there is an enormous animal of some sort in Tasisuak Lake. Lying to the north and extending west from Nain for 90 kilometres, this body of water continues as the Fraser River for another 60 kilometres to the Quebec border; it is big enough to hide dozens of such monsters. Since the lake is only a kilometre wide, one would think most travellers would much rather cross it than go around it. However, the resident beast is said to have many arms, and travellers in canoe or walking on clear ice are often enveloped by it and dragged down into the depths. Ritchie added that every time he has had occasion to cross the lake he has kept to snow-covered ice and has never ventured there in a canoe.

Longtime resident Edward Voisey backed Ritchie up, saying that his father, Antoine Noah, knew of a long-necked creature that was seen only at certain times in the summer or fall. Voisey added that, while he had never seen anything

Cressie, according to area residents; the "replica" near the lake is for the benefit of unbelievers.

uncommon in the lake, the Innu swore there was some strange creature there, possibly a variety of giant squid.[10]

Perhaps the province's best-known cryptid is the creature reputed to dwell in Crescent Lake near Robert's Arm. The area has been inhabited since about 1850, and something or other has generated numerous tales over the years. Running southwest of and behind the community, Route 380 follows the lake's twisting, eight-kilometre-long north shore; it is generally from this road that our variant of Nessie and her kin are seen. Cressie (*Cressiteras angulloida*, a pseudo-scientific name) has long caused some consternation in the region; evidence of the beast can be traced to native legends, possibly Algonquian or even Beothuk, which referred to the *woodum haoot* (pond demon) or *haoot tuwedyee* (swimming demon).

The first modern report is said to come from around 1900 when a Grandmother Anthony, who was picking berries near the lake, returned home and launched into an unbelievable tale. She had spotted a huge serpentine creature swimming about the lake, the like of which she had never imagined, much less seen, before.

Alas, there were only wavelets of interest, and nothing further was seen or heard of the thing (or at least nothing was recorded) until mid-century when the first of a score or so of reports was made. All had seen a black or dark-brown snake-like creature seven or eight metres long. Some residents armed themselves and patrolled the shores of the lake for weeks.

A plaque on the shoreline tells how in the 1950s (others say in 1945) a pair of local loggers saw what they thought was a stray broom-stick just off shore. The fact that it was drifting against the wind aroused their curiosity and they headed their boat toward it. Suddenly, the eight-metre-long log, black and rounded, slipped beneath the surface. One of the men, Andrew Burton, recalled that they wasted little time getting back to shore.

Another significant sighting took place on June 7, 1960, when Bruce Anthony and three other loggers watched an object they thought to be an overturned boat – that is, until it swam along near the shore and crossed a sandbar.[11] The story was expanded upon by another source which stated that a giant conger eel was seen by four loggers as it bored its way *through* a sand bank in the summer of 1960.[12] There are no other details, but boring through a sandbar seems out of character for a conger eel.

Some believe the creatures are abnormally large freshwater eels (*Anguilloidei*), which several luckless RCMP divers had the dubious pleasure of twice encountering. During winter, mysterious holes sometimes occur in the ice on the lake, and because of their size they have been mistaken for sites where snowmobiles have accidentally broken through. In the early 1980s, divers were called in to investigate one of these holes, but they turned up nothing except the fact that there was something down there, and the holes seemed to have been made by an object coming out of the lake rather than going into it.

Several years later, while attempting to recover a body from a downed plane, others believe they met eels as big around as a teakettle, which set upon them. The divers returned to shore somewhat shaken but uninjured. These events are unsubstantiated by the police, but if they did meet such things, it is unlikely they were what we usually think of when we consider eels.

Another man from Robert's Arm reported seeing a "slim black shape" rise a metre-and-a-half from a patch of agitated water before it sank from sight. Not only did his report make the front page of several local newspapers, it even appeared in *The Augusta Chronicle*, Georgia.[13]

On July 9, 1991, at about noon, retired Robert's Arm schoolteacher and newspaper correspondent Fred Parsons and his wife saw what they believed to be some sort of animal on the surface of the lake. It was dark brown, an estimated six metres long, and swam with an up-and-down motion, as would a mammal.[14] Parsons, recipient of the Robert's Arm Citizen of the Year Award, is considered to be a particularly reliable witness.

That fall, on September 5, as local resident Pierce Rideout drove his pickup truck along the lakeshore, he saw what appeared to be the bow wave of a small boat about 150 metres from shore, between Warr's Service Station and the forested point of land on the far side of the lake.

At that moment, the slowly moving object submerged, but as he watched, it came up again, and the three or four-metre-long black shape pitched forward in a rolling motion as it swam, much as a whale or other mammal does. There was no sign of fin, tail, or fluke, nor did he see its neck (perhaps all that he saw was "neck"). Then the shape sank from sight.

Rideout unabashedly allowed that he had derided tales of a monster in Crescent Lake only a few days earlier, but his position had changed somewhat.[15] The matter-of-fact farmer and part-time mailman was so troubled by it that he began carrying a gun when necessity had him travelling near the lake.[16]

Russell Bragg, a writer from the area, noted that in 1995

the RCMP had possibly discovered related eel-like creatures while investigating a drowning in South Pond, a similar-sized lake not far away. However, corroborating evidence has not been found.[17]

For a while, no one saw Cressie, and there were those who wondered if she had died or moved on. But at the beginning of July 2000, Robbie Watkins and Richard Goudie were part of a crew working along the Hazelnut Hiking Trail when they spotted what they believe to have been the elusive beast.

After another leave of absence, the original and unclassifiable animal seemed to be back at its old haunts in 2003. On August 14, the CBC released a report from Vivian Short, also of Robert's Arm, who claimed to have seen it. Short was one of those who paid little attention to the foolishness surrounding Crescent Lake and its monster – until, while driving with a friend, she rounded a bend in the road and there it stood, more or less. Her description was of a serpentine creature with a fishlike head. The genuine article!

Said Short, "I was just a' screamin' 'We saw Cressie! We saw Cressie!' Excited, eh? 'Well,' I said to my friend, 'Oh my! That's big! That could eat four or five people if they were swimmin', like.'"

Robert's Arm town clerk Ada Rowsell said Short was not the only one to see Cressie around that time. "I've had several reports of people sighting some kind of a huge monster or sea serpent or some kind of a fish."[18] Someone also reported that eels "thicker than a man's thigh" were photographed in the depths of the lake, while others said that several were killed and taken away for examination, but these tales have never been confirmed.[19]

William Clarke, of the Robert's Arm newspaper *Nor'wester*, reported on June 18, 2008, that Cressie was going to have a chance to appear on the History Channel. CMJ Productions, an independent company specializing in documentaries, was in town for the express purpose of capturing the uncooperative

Cressie for television's popular programme *Monster Quest*. CMJ's director Leo Singer said, "We've been looking and we've been using all kinds of interesting techniques trying to find something and we've got some interesting results."[20]

The programme *Lake Monsters of the North* aired on September 17, bringing Cressie back into the limelight. Mayor Daphne Parsons candidly acknowledged that she hoped it would increase their tourist trade.

Some think Cressie may be an oversized American eel (*Anguilla rostrata*); these are normally between one and two metres long and usually spawn in the ocean. Even so, they have never been seen in Tommy's Arm Brook, Crescent Lake's only outlet to the sea, which is about three kilometres distant. While the lake's deeper water is saline, which may allow eels to stay in the lake and breed there, it is most improbable.

There has been some disparity in the estimated length of the anomalous creature – from one-and-a-half up to eight

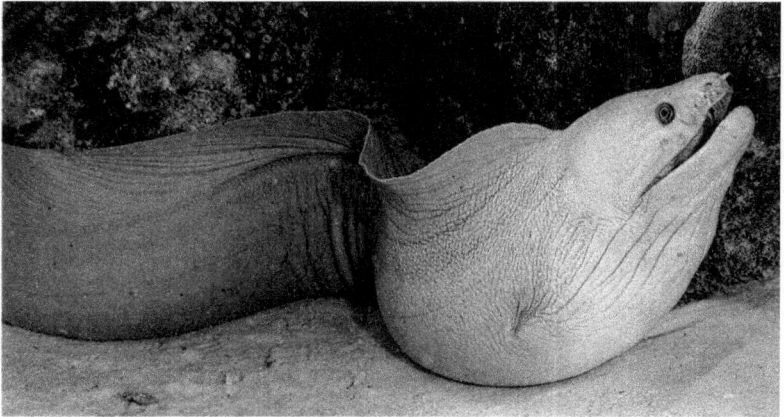

The moray is not unknown in Newfoundland waters and often attains a length of two metres or more.

metres – which led many to suggest there may be a family of the lake dwellers. Of course, a solitary animal could hardly be expected to live here for two hundred years or to reproduce.

An undulating mode of swimming would preclude Cressie being an eel: the up-and-down fashion is, as previously mentioned, definitely mammalian. Eels, on the other hand, are bottom-dwelling creatures, and their swimming motions, as with all fish, are from side to side. Sightings also invariably occur during the day whereas eels are more or less nocturnal.

Some believe the study of such creatures may lead to the discovery of a new species of eel, but we already know of adult eels that have reached six metres in length. Moreover, in the early 1930s, Danish marine biologists discovered a deep sea eel larva two metres long; as an adult, this fish could exceed an immoderate 18 metres in length.

Tales of Cressie persist, and though there are no known photographs, descriptions from first-hand accounts are remark-ably alike – dark, eel-like, sometimes showing a rounded hump, without noticeable fins or flukes, and swimming with an undulating motion.[21]

Dr. Joe Nickell, Senior Research Fellow of the Committee for Skeptical Inquiry, believes there is a dark-coloured creature that swims both underwater and on the surface, where its wake can make it appear much longer, and it moves in an undulating manner: the northern river otter. Otters swimming in a line, and they may infrequently do so, could give the effect of a single, long, serpentine creature making its way through the water, but this seems to be grasping at straws in an effort to identify our perplexing friend.

Whatever is lurking in Crescent Lake is large and is one of the more plausible of North American lake cryptids. Some skeptics, though, have wondered whether there really is a Cressie or if the story is just a gimmick to boost tourism. A few have gone so far as to quote Mayor Parsons as "proof" of this, and a fanciful model of Cressie stands beside the lake with a sign proclaiming, "Welcome to Robert's Arm. Beothuk Trail. Lake Monster Country. The Loch Ness of Newfoundland." Admittedly, to date no one has achieved immortality by photographing Cressie, the most famous of our lake monsters, or by becoming its dinner.

There may be yet another unusual creature in one of our lakes. Recently a credible and lucid account came from an individual who, understandably, would rather not see his name in print. Granted, some who know this witness have described him as one who dispenses the truth with great economy and has the most riotous of imaginations. However, it is difficult to say that he is any better or worse than most other informants.

While fishing the 100-kilometre-long, 300-metre-deep Grand Lake, he was drifting along the shoreline some distance south of Howley, interested solely in the land-locked salmon residing there. Some wisps of fog lingered on this calm and quiet morning. He happened to glance over his right shoulder and was taken aback by what appeared to be a large horse-like or camel-like head supported by a long slender neck projecting from the water. The head swivelled about, baseball-sized eyes calmly inspecting its surroundings until they came to rest on him. Slowly the neck retreated into the water until the head finally submerged, the eyeballs being the last to disappear, soundlessly and with scarcely a ripple. He said it was not terrifying in the least, but markedly eerie.[22]

There have also been rumours of an odd lake creature putting in an appearance in one of the province's Dildo Ponds at some recent time. Despite an assiduous attempt to track down the origin of this tale, nothing has been found, and if this was the Dildo Pond at Blaketown, nothing has been seen there despite a decade of fishing derbies. In attempting to obtain more information one may also discover that even the Internet is of little use in this regard; it is surprising (or perhaps not) what pops up when one searches "Monster Dildo Newfoundland."

1. Henry W. LeMessurier, *A Lecture on Placentia* – March 1910 (St. John's, NL: Centre for Newfoundland Studies, MUN), 14–15.

2. "Pepamuteiati Nitassinat: As We Walk Across Our Land," Innu Nation and Sheshatshiu Innu First Nation, accessed August 17, 2010, http://www.innuplaces.ca/fiche.php?id = 332&lang = en.

3. Jonathan Maberry, *Vampire Universe* (New York: The Citadel Press, 2006), 283.

4. "Manitutshu the Spirit Mountain at Muskrat Falls," Innu Nation Website, accessed October 18, 2009, http://web.archive.org/web/20071015175019/http://innu.ca/muskrat.html.

5. Innu Traditional Knowledge Committee, *Environmental Knowledge of the Mishta-shipu* (Churchill River) Area, Proposed Lower Churchill Project (St. John's, NL: Peter Armitage / Wolverine & Associates Inc., June 20, 2007), 94–96.

6. Ibid.

7. John S. R. Gosse, *Whitbourne – Newfoundland's First Inland Town* (Whitbourne, NL: J. S. R. Gosse, 1985), 114.

8. George M. Eberhart, *Mysterious Creatures: A Guide to Cryptozoology* (Santa Barbara, CA: ABC-CLIO, 2002), 308; X, "*A mari usque ad mare,*" *Fortean Times*, no. 46 (Spring 1986), 44–51.

9. F. W. L. Peacock & L. Jackson, *Reflections From a Snowhouse* (St. John's, NL: Jesperson Press, 1986), 98.

10. *Them Days*, Happy Valley-Goose Bay, NL, Vol. 2 (Winter 1997), 110.

11. John Braddock, "Monsters of the Maritimes," *Atlantic Advocate* 58 (January 1968), 12–17.

12. Benjamin Radford & Joe Nickell, *Lake Monster Mysteries* (Lexington, KY: University Press of Kentucky, 2006), 89–99.

13. E. Randall Floyd, "Cressie of Crescent Lake – A Monster Eel?" *The Augusta Chronicle* (Augusta, GA), March 21, 1999.

14. Radford & Nickell, *Lake Monster Mysteries*, 189–99.

15. Eberhart, *Mysterious Creatures*, 114.

16. Floyd, *Augusta Chronicle*, March 21, 1999.

17. Radford & Nickell, *Lake Monster Mysteries*,189–99.

18. *CBC News*, CBC News Online Staff, August 14, 2003.

19. Floyd, *The Augusta Chronicle*, March 21, 1999.

20. William Clarke, "Big cat concerns prompt official reaction." *Nor'wester*, (Springdale, NL), November 6, 2008.

21. Braddock, *Atlantic Advocate*, 12–17.

22. Anonymous, personal communication, 2005.

chapter
five

MAN *of* THE FOREST

Known around the world by various names, the "sasquatch" or "bigfoot," according to one hypothesis, is North America's great ape. This possibility has been raised as a logical explanation for the evidence and reports collected in many parts of the continent over the past two centuries. The name sasquatch is from the Salish people of the Canadian West Coast – their word *se'sxac* means "wild men," and in the United States the more common term is "bigfoot." For our purposes we will use "sasquatch." In many respects these creatures resemble the *yeti* or abominable snowman of the Himalayas, the *almas* of Siberia, the *yowie* of Australia, and the *hibagon* or "mountain man" of Japan.

It has been suggested that sasquatch might be a surviving population of *Gigantopithecus* that crossed the land bridge now occupied by the Bering Strait, although no archaeological or anthropological evidence has been found to support this theory. Other researchers have suggested that the giant, hairy creatures might be under alien control or might themselves be aliens.[1]

This creature, described as apelike, was said to have been captured in Saxony around 1530.

Shades of Chewbacca! This UFO connection is one of the more bizarre and intriguing aspects of the sasquatch mystery.

According to cryptozoologist Dr. Karl Shuker, the creature's face is typically described as apelike, with a sloping brow, prominent eyebrow ridges, light-reflecting eyes (usually a nocturnal adaptation), a broad flattened nose, and a lipless slit of a mouth. It is said to have a powerful, muscular chest, very long arms, pawlike hands with thick fingers and hairless palms, sturdy muscular legs, and no tail.

Upright, its height ranges from 150 to 275 centimetres (in a few cases heights of nearly four metres have been reported!). Though it commonly has an awkward bipedal gait, it sometimes runs on all fours and has a strong putrid odour. Its hair, usually reddish-brown to black, is about 15 to 20 centimetres long, and its calls are moans, grunts, howls, and high-pitched shrieks. Reports of the sasquatch's reaction to humans run the gamut from benignity to aggressiveness, including attacks and even a few kidnappings. Primarily nocturnal it shows interest in, but has no fear of, human dwellings, although reportedly it dislikes cats and dogs intensely.[2]

Based on the many descriptions of gorillalike and apelike beings, the author of *The Sasquatch File*, *On the Track of the Sasquatch*, *Year of the Sasquatch*, and *Sasquatch: The Apes Among Us*, John Green has referred to it as an ape since the 1960s. And one-time skeptic Dr. John A. Bindernagel, a British-Columbian wildlife biologist and author of *North America's Great Ape: The Sasquatch*, has been considering the evidence for such a creature since 1963.[3] One of many studying the elusive creature, Bindernagel is satisfied that the sasquatch is a real animal, and, furthermore, he is quite certain he saw one in 2007. Based on a purely scientific approach, he is convinced the beast exists and should be subject to study and examination like any other large mammal. World-famous English primatologist and scientist Dr. Jane Goodall took a firm stance on the subject when she commented on Dr. Bindernagel's work during an interview on National Public Radio (PBS) on September 27, 2002: "I find it exciting that, finally, a book has been written that accepts the existence of the Sasquatch and carefully describes the behavioural characteristics that have been recorded."

Admittedly, plaster casts of footprints are the only solid evidence we have for the sasquatch's existence, but wildlife biologists routinely depend on tracks as evidence of the presence of wildlife. Tracks offer a more reliable and lasting proof of its existence than do fleeting glimpses of the beast itself or photographs, film, and videos that are commonly considered to have been fabricated.

Does Newfoundland and Labrador have its own small colony of these creatures? In his book, *Manlike Monsters on Trial: Early Records and Modern Evidence*, Michael Taft points out that there are no local Newfoundland traditions distinctly identifying sasquatch-like creatures, but occasionally people describe encounters with hairy beings in or near the forest. Not surprisingly, they prefer to place such things in more culturally acceptable categories such as spirits, the devil, fairies, or as nothing more than bears.

A more-or-less typical portrayal of sasquatch.

Our northernmost residents, the Inuit ("the people"), differentiate themselves, at least to their own satisfaction, from both bears and the legendary *Tuniit* (singular *Tuniq*). They consider the *Tuniit* a separate and fabulous race, while at the same time regarding them as their ancestors. Some researchers think the name may refer to the earlier Dorset culture (800 bce – 1,000 ce) of the Arctic.[4] In any case, they believe the *Tuniit* have dwelt in that land long before today's residents put in an appearance, and the whole is left open to conjecture.

The *Tuniit* were thought to have inhabited the Torngat Mountains of northern Labrador and the area along the Hudson Strait; they were personified as huge white bears and reputedly occupied a great cave. All the same, at other times they were said to have resided among the Inuit in large stone houses, and what are said to be ruins of these buildings are still pointed out with some awe by today's residents.

The Inuit also told of unfavourable encounters with these "devils" or "spirits." Vastly taller and stronger than the Inuit, and with very long arms and legs, they stole such things that they could not make. Many an Inuit bow or kayak was acquired by these unclassified hominoids, the owners being indisposed to resist. The *Tuniit* did, however, make and use stone implements.[5]

According to Inuit legend, this stupid and slow-going race was hunted to extinction by the Thule culture (more recent antecedents of today's Inuit) some centuries before the coming of Europeans.[6] Even so, possibly some *Tuniit* escaped this early ethnic cleansing and may have survived into the 1930s. Others, among them cryptozoologist Mark Hall, suggest these subarctic ape-men may be a totally different hominoid group from that which we call the North American sasquatch or bigfoot.[7]

A number of these giant human-like creatures were said to have once lived at Saglek, well north of Hebron; one was apparently so well known to the Inuit that they referred to him by his proper name of *Sikuliak Siuyutuk*. Tales of this being, passed down over the years, are familiar to the Inuit to this day.[8]

Kaminaushit-natuashu, 50 kilometres west-southwest of Nain, is known to the Innu as Hairy Creature Lake. One time, a man hunting here disappeared along with his dog team and *komatik*. No trace was found of him or his dogs, and others were warned to avoid the place, presumably because of the presence of a hairy and evil being.

Less than a dozen kilometres to the east of Hairy Creature Lake, and not far from Emish (i.e., Voisey's Bay), stands *Kaminaushit upishkutinam*, or Hairy Creature Mountain. Known today as Makhavinekh Mountain, folktales relate that long ago an Innu saw a human-like creature on this promontory. It was hairy, large, and threatening, and the observer made great haste to leave the area that stands, to this day, as a monument to what may be a vanished race.

According to traditional Innu history, their country was peopled with numerous beings, other than humans, not so very long ago. Some of these stories originate with the Innu *kamanitushit* (shamans) who brokered relations between the Innu and these probable sub-humans. The *Akamiuapishku* (Mealy Mountains) territory contains a number of special places where such bipeds have been seen. Some, such as *Meminteu* and *Aatshen*, were extremely dangerous and cannibals to boot. They were to be avoided at all times, and fortunately, were rather scarce. Others were relatively benign, given their space and a little respect.

Tales of encounters were passed down from generation to generation and now reside with today's elders. Such fauna, if we may call them that, were primarily met by shamans or elders who were performing the shaking tent (*kushapatshikan*) ceremony. The last shamans from the Sheshatshiu area were Shinipesht Pokue (aka *Uatshitshish*) and Atuan Ashini (aka *Uashuaunnu*), both closely associated with the Mealy Mountains. *Uashuaunnu* made his last shaking tent in their shadows, and it may be that shamans had a vested interest in propagating such tales.

The *Uapanatsheu*, or "sneaking creatures," were skulkers, usually invisible, with a habit of stealing from traps and throwing stones and sticks at the Innu tents. Naturally, the body of water known as *Uapanatsheu-nipi*, or Sneaking Creature Lake, 80 kilometres southeast of Happy Valley-Goose Bay, was named because of their presence. *Uapanatsheu-shipiss*, Sneaking Creature River, flows from the lake.

Beside this lake, a hundred or more years ago, a dog treed a sneaking creature near an Innu camp. Delivering whatever sort of beast it was from the dog, the people determined to keep it alive. Subsequently, it lived with Lizette Penashue's unidentified great-great-grandmother. The old camping area was called *Kanutshikatsheht katshimaitsheshuat*, and this has been interpreted as "Where sneaking creatures were bothersome." Apparently, they were especially so when it was foggy.

Interestingly, there is another Sneaking Creature Lake, shown on maps as Cabot Lake, 155 kilometres north-north-west of Happy Valley-Goose Bay, where the local *Uapanatsheu* and Point Revenge cultures were said to be quite similar to humans.

Memekueshu, or "cave creatures," were a subterranean race who, like the sneaking creatures, have been reported by Innu from all over the Labrador-Quebec peninsula and by the James Bay Cree, close relatives of the Innu.

Beaver Brook Pond, south of Lake Melville in the Mealy Mountains, is said to be the site of another confrontation. A group of Innu paddled to the end of the pond where a door in the side of the mountain opened to reveal a cave from which music emanated. Unfortunately, it was inhabited by cave creatures, and when one Innu behaved in a manner considered offensive by the irascible denizens, a chase resulted. Luckily, the Innu made good their escape, but since then they have referred to that body of water as *Memekueshu-nipi*, or Cave Creature Lake. Coincidentally, just to the northwest and about a dozen kilometres away lies *Manitupeku*, Evil Creature Lake, where the monster resembling a giant beaver beetle dwelt.

Is it possible that some of these beings were related in some manner to the *skrælings* of Norse history? It has been cemented in the minds of sociologists and archaeologists that this was the term Norse adventurers used when referring to natives of their newly found lands, chief among them the Dorset, Thule, and Point Revenge cultures.

It is likely that the first time Europeans met a bigfoot or one of his relatives was around 986 ce, when the wayfaring Leif Eriksson and his fellow Norsemen arrived at L'Anse aux Meadows. Included in his account of the voyage was his encounter with hairy forest-dwellers of mythic proportions. According to Eriksson, they were much larger than members of his crew, most of whom could not be considered small for the time. He claimed their foul smell was worse than their terrible visage and their horrid and deafening screams.

An authoritative book called *The Norse Discovery of America* carries the following description of a meeting with strangers, but it is doubtful that these were what we understand to be *skrælings*:

> They saw a great number of skin-canoes, and staves were brandished from the boats, with a noise like flails...There-upon the strangers rowed toward them, and went upon the land, marvelling at those whom they saw before them. They were swarthy men and ill-looking, and the hair of their heads was ugly. They had great eyes, and were broad of cheek. They tarried there for a time looking curiously at the people they saw before them, and then rowed away, and to the southward around the point.[9]

Peter Byrne conceded in *The Search for Bigfoot: Monster, Myth or Man?* that it is more probable the creatures they encountered were simply natives. He contends that the Norse word *skræling* (used to describe these creatures or people) in fact means "barbarian." However, he admits that he is puzzled by their description of *skrælings* as particularly big and hairy, since the Norse themselves were distinctly big and hairy. In addition, the statement regarding their "great eyes" is confusing, as it fits no natives of today. As if in support of Byrne's bewilderment, the *History of Norway*, in all likelihood dating to the mid-1200s, states:

> [F]arther to the north, hunters have come across small people, whom they call Skrælings; when they are hit their wounds turn white and they do not bleed, but when they die there is no end to their bleeding. They possess no iron, but use walrus tusk for missiles and sharpened stones instead of knives.[10]

Since Eriksson also mentioned the Beothuk separately from the belligerent *skrælings*, they were doubtless something entirely different. Evidently, the Norse had several meetings with the "hairy men" before leaving. Note though, the *skrælings* had a boat, which is quite un-bigfoot-like; also, they were large, whereas the *skrælings* of *The Greenlanders' Saga* were "earth dwarves." These latter were said to be a race of warlike pygmies who badgered the Vikings, around 1,000 ce, when the latter undertook to establish settlements in the New World.

Gerardus Mercator added the word *skrælings* to his map of the unexplored northern regions in 1569, and Sigurd Stefánsson's map of 1570 shows a large peninsula which he labelled *Skrælingeland*, otherwise known as *Promontorium Winlandia*, near the Labrador coast and which we now call the Great Northern Peninsula. It should be recognized, however, that the word *skræling* did not appear until a couple hundred years after the Vinland visits.

The Thule people, ancestors of today's Inuit, first arrived in Greenland from the North American mainland in the 13th century; soon they were known to the Norse of Greenland as *skrælings*. When *The Greenlanders' Saga* and *The Saga of Erik the Red* were written, the term was "backdated" to refer to the natives of Vinland. This is possibly the only word surviving from the Old Norse dialect, and in today's Icelandic, *skrælingi* (plural *skrælingar*) means "barbarian" or "foreigner."[11]

William H. Babcock, in *Certain Pre-Columbian Notices of American Aborigines*, writes that the word *skræling* may have been the name of one of the North American tribes encountered by the Norse during initial contact. As evidence he cites a traditional story of Bjorn the Bonde who rescued a pair of *skrælings*, a brother and sister, from the sea. It was their custom to show gratitude by becoming their rescuer's life-long servants, and so Bjorn found himself the object of their utmost concern and affection. The two disclosed that the word *skræling* was how the Norse pronounced the name of their people. Sadly, when the pair were forbidden to accompany Bjorn on his return to Iceland, they threw themselves off a cliff to their deaths.

In this province, the prototypical ape-man was frequently reckoned by the Innu and Inuit to be an ancestral ghost of sorts. More recent local stories, not necessarily native tales, tell of a large creature covered with hair that is met with abruptly when one's attention is elsewhere.[12]

What are we to make of the horrific and unidentified beasts in the legend of Marguerite de la Rocque's sojourn on the Isle of Demons, generally thought to have been Belle Isle? In 1542, Jean-François de La Rocque, Sieur de Roberval, set out for Quebec where he was to found a colony. His company consisted of an assortment of peasants, adventurers, ne'er-do-wells, servants, soldiers, and even some of noble birth, among them the beauteous young Marguerite, said to be his niece. In spite of Jean-François' objections, Marguerite became passionately involved with a young man of the company, whose name is unrecorded. Furious at her persistence, de La Rocque had her marooned on the island with her aged nurse Damienne, her anonymous lover, a small amount of food, and six arquebuses. Left to their own devices, the trio set up a makeshift shelter and endeavoured to find something to sustain themselves. The demons were at their very worst shortly after their arrival, and the trio were tormented nearly beyond endurance. Manifold fiends wailed and ripped at the interlopers' pathetic hut but could not get in. When the girl became pregnant, the malicious brutes proved perverse and troublesome beyond belief, but still the marooned lovers resisted. The nervy girl shot three white bears that loitered about their camp one day, but against demons, bullets were of little use.

As the weeks dragged by, various monstrosities killed Marguerite's child, maid, and her young man. Alone, she was faced with imps and spirits that peered out of the mist, whispered in the night, and called and whistled in the gale. These evil ones had wings and horned heads, and they howled like a crowd in the marketplace, confused and inarticulate. Vessels, seeing signs of activity on the haunted island, gave it a wide berth. Finally, after two-and-a-half years, the crew of a fishing vessel saw smoke and despite trepidations rescued the girl and returned her to France.[13]

André Thévet (1516–1590), French explorer, author, and cosmographer.

Seamen had known of the dreadful *Isola de Demoni* for many years. Indeed, the entire Labrador coast was acknowledged to be overrun by such appalling creatures; the island was regarded as the prime domain of the most evil of these fiends and devils. Sixteenth-century historian Father André

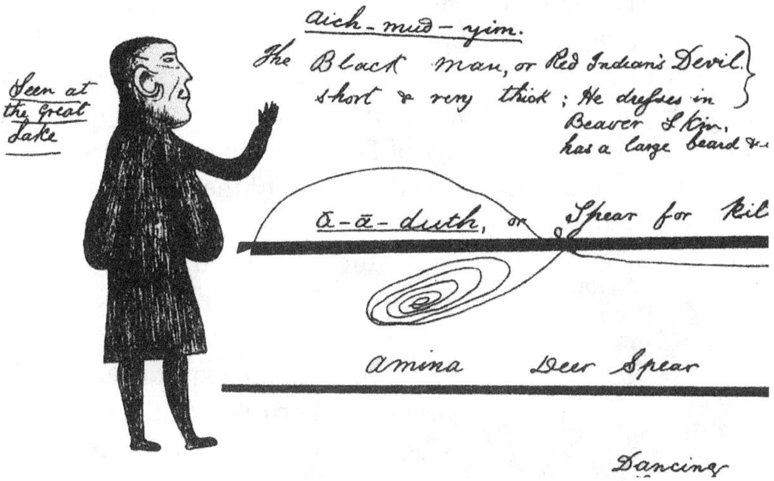
Aich-mud-yim.
The Black man, or Red Indian's Devil.
short & very thick; He dresses in
Beaver Skin,
has a large beard
Seen at the Great Lake
ā-ā-duth, or Spear for Kil
amina Deer Spear
Dancing

The Black Man of Red Indian Lake.

Thévet told of seeing the resident fiends torturing the natives until they were forced to seek relief from the good priest himself. He, contradictorily, portrayed the creatures as fine-looking but so malevolent that the natives were compelled to leave.

What could these creatures have been? Merely wolves? Marguerite would have recognized wolves at once, as they were quite common in Europe. Certainly they were not bears, as she acknowledged having killed at least three of these; besides, what could be more threatening or frightening than a polar bear? Is it more likely they were demons or some creatures unknown to her? Were they related to the beings identified variously as yeti, sasquatch, and bigfoot? While that may not seem reasonable, it is at least possible.

While Shanadithit, a Beothuk, lived with William Cormack at St. John's in the winter of 1829, she told him that the spirit world of her people included – besides the workaday Great Spirit – a creature called *Aich-mud-yim*, or Black Man, sometimes referred to as the "Red Indian Devil" by Europeans. She produced a picture of this being, whom she described as short and very thick, dressed in beaver skin, and having a long beard. Yet, as Howley pointed out in his book, her drawing shows an individual without any sort of facial adornment. She said this mysterious hominid lived on the shores of the Great Lake, now known as Red Indian Lake.[14]

Joseph Michelin around 1910.

Much later in the 19th century, around 1895, William Decker, a resident of one of the numerous small settlements at the extreme end of the Great Northern Peninsula, set out on a hunting trip one winter morning. He trekked into the boggy southwest hinterlands of Pistolet Bay, and when halfway across a frozen quagmire, he was startled by an unearthly cry. Turning, he was horrified to see what he later called an immense "beast-man" charging toward him in tremendous bounds. Hastily he knelt and with trembling hands simply pointed his muzzle-loader at the thing – now perilously close – and pulled the trigger.

The heavy charge brought the creature down, but it struggled to its feet again, barely giving Decker time to ready another load. He fired again and the beast fell so close to him that he could smell its foetid breath. Taking no chances, Decker rammed in another charge and shot into the twisting body a third time as it lay on the snowy ground.

Satisfied it was dead, Decker took some rough measurements. It was from three to three-and-a-half-metres tall with an arm span of more than four metres. He estimated its weight at around 450 kilograms. It was covered with long dark hair, and Decker found his snowshoes were too small to cover the huge tracks it had left in the snow. His description is unquestionably familiar.

Leaving his late antagonist where it lay, Decker wasted no time in leaving the area. Some have suggested that this might have been the last of the Newfoundland sasquatches, but there have been other and more recent reports.[15] There was a rumour of another hairy being, more than two metres tall, having been killed in Newfoundland sometime after 1901, but little has been found other than the one obscure mention.

A better-known case is said to have taken place in 1908 along Labrador's Traverspine River, known to the Innu as *Manatueu-shipiss*, and a tributary of the Churchill. There was considerable excitement here when women saw an animal or a being resembling a huge hairy man.

In the fall of 1909, Yale University's John Rowland and a small crew of students took the auxiliary ketch *Yale* from Boston to Labrador for the Grenfell Mission. After their arrival, one of their duties was to make a run every two weeks to the head of Hamilton Inlet (where the Happy Valley-Goose Bay airport is now situated) to pick up mail. The next spring, they took advantage of one of these trips to explore the bay itself and look for traces of the mysterious beast said to live in the area.

Several livyer families were there, and though no one admitted to having actually seen the monster in daylight, the descriptions they gave were all similar. Taller than a man and with an exceptionally long neck, it whistled or snorted when alarmed and was very fast on its feet. Accompanied by what appeared to be a young monster, the beasts ravaged the livyers' sparse gardens. Its "slipper-shaped" tracks were unlike that of any known animal – that is, without a pronounced heel and roughly the size of a man's foot. Furthermore, the tracks sank about five centimetres into compacted sand where a big man could scarcely make an impression with the heel of his boot, indicating considerable weight.[16]

Edward C. Robinson, FGS, visited Labrador in 1907–1908 and published his book, *In An Unknown Land*, in 1909. One chapter, which he misleadingly called "On the trail of the mammoth," told of an unusual Labrador native that may be extinct today. He declared that, while he would not vouch for the verity of detail, he was convinced they were factual. Residents of the area thoroughly believed they had seen and heard a variant of gorilla, while others said, somewhat furtively and reluctantly, that they believed it was the Devil. Robinson was certain of one thing: There was no desire among the locals to gain publicity nor to deceive him. They stated their case simply and succinctly.[17]

Joseph Michelin, born at Rigolet in 1846, was a chief witness to these events. A hunter and trapper of great repute, he had found the trail of a mysterious animal near the Traverspine, unusual in itself for this knowledgeable woodsman. The long footprints had but two toes, and the maker of the tracks must have been uncommonly heavy as its feet had sunk deeply into earth where a man would leave hardly a trace. The visitor seemed to be bipedal and its stride substantially longer than a metre. Michelin followed the prints along the bank of the river, which was low at the time, for many kilometres. The few inhabitants about made their way to the river to have a look – the odd trail disturbed them greatly.

One night shortly thereafter, Michelin's wife, Mary, was at home alone when she heard a rumbling sort of whistling sound, like heavy breathing. Now and then tree branches snapped. She quietly took a rifle down from its rack, loaded it, and stepped outside. She found the dogs, which would tackle a bear, close beside the cabin shaking with fright. It was too dark to see anything clearly so she fired a shot at random into the woods; abruptly there came the sound of something heavy crashing hurriedly through the trees. The dogs refused the chase and skulked about near the door as she entered the house and barred it.

Next day, in the afternoon, her husband returned from downstream with a friend. After listening to Mary's story, the men accompanied her into the woods and found that some enormous beast had been there. Following its tracks down to the river, they found where it had gone straight into the water, thereby ending the possibility of pursuit. There had evidently been two of them: Beside the larger tracks were smaller but similar footprints less than a metre apart. They thought it was likely a mother and her young.

World traveller and author Lionel Leslie detailed his 1928 Labrador adventures in his book *Wilderness Trails in Three Continents: An Account of Travel, Big Game Hunting and Exploration in India, Burma, China, East Africa and Labrador.* He told of children playing along the Traverspine River being badly frightened in 1913 when they spied a grotesque face peering at them from willows along the riverbank. One girl described it as an enormous hairy thing more than two metres in height when standing upright, but at times moving about on all fours. It had long arms, a white crest, and showed white teeth when it grinned. When it beckoned to her, she and the others ran screaming to the house and told their elders.

This may well be a revised version of the previous tale, as one of the youngsters was a grandchild of Joseph Michelin, who lived nearby. Joe was away, but his wife grabbed up a shot-gun and went to investigate. Through the brush she saw an indistinct figure and knowing at once it was neither a neighbour nor a passing Innu, fired both barrels. While this was enough to convince the visitor to stay away during the day, tracks indicated it returned at night. Their pattern was recorded, and, like previous tracks, they were about 30 centimetres long with a narrow heel and deep impressions showing two rounded toes.

Leslie said he had met a group of trappers who unsuccess-fully attempted to hunt the thing down. While they did not find their anticipated quarry, the trappers were certain the women saw exactly what they said they saw. He speculated that the natives' belief in the Windigo may have influenced or excited their imagination, but he still thought the vast wilderness perhaps held some creatures never seen by white men.[18] He wrote:

> The widespread belief in the Windigo exists in Labrador as it does throughout the North, even as far as Alaska. This Windigo is a frightful hairy man at least fifteen feet [4.5 metres] in height who lives on the flesh of human beings. Any particularly large or peculiar tracks in the snow are accredited to the monster. This superstition forcibly reminded me of a similar one which exists amongst the Tibetans – their Abominable Snowman.[19]

The Windigo – a staple in the culture and traditions of numerous North American tribes – were giant cannibals who roamed the northeastern woods in the dead of winter and devoured any humans they found. They have been further described in "myth" as a manlike atrocity with bones nearly protruding through its desiccated grey hide, sunken glowing eyes, bloody lips, a slimy tongue, and sharp yellow fangs – it may be up to six or seven metres in height and has an odour similar to that of rotting flesh.

This malicious cannibal can also take possession of human bodies, and those who yield to cannibalism are apt to become a Windigo. Indeed, it is said that the only way one could escape its grasp was to turn into a Windigo as well and fight the monster on its own terms. Many attribute the loss of hunters and travellers to members of this voracious tribe.[20]

Elliott "Bud" Merrick was a WOP, a worker without pay, at the Grenfell Mission in 1929 and stayed on as a teacher in the town of North West River. He became a close a friend of John Michelin with whom he made a 480-kilometre canoe trip and trek into the interior. In his book, *True North*, Merrick called the entity the "Traverspine Gorilla" and told of it using a stick as a weapon and feeding upon grubs rooted from rotten logs and the bark of trees. The depth of its tracks indicated its weight, which was thought to be something in excess of 225 kilograms. Apparently it prowled around the small settlement for two consecutive winters, terrifying residents.[21]

In his memoirs, Dr. Harry L. Paddon wrote that the creature had a mate, since two sets of tracks were found together. In addition, what sounded like quarrelling was sometimes accompanied by loud wails from what was presumed to be the smaller of the two. The tracks and noise provoked a search of monumental proportions. Residents set up a watch at night, and some loggers working at Mud Lake began a hunt for it, but they had no luck.[22]

Philip H. Godsell (1889–1961), who had spent many years with the Hudson Bay Company and had studied the wildlife of Eastern Canada, came across this queer tale in Merrick's book and decided to look into it. He was well qualified to do so, having produced many books, short stories, articles, and radio broadcasts predominantly about his experiences in the North. At North West River he met some of the people mentioned in the story, who recalled the considerable commotion around Traverspine at that time.[23]

The case particularly intrigued New Brunswick biologist Dr. Bruce Stanley Wright, who was also familiar with Merrick's account, and he went to investigate for himself in 1947. Wright's credentials were impeccable. During World War II, he had formed and commanded the Royal Canadian Navy's Sea Reconnaissance Unit, later writing *The Frogmen of Burma* based on his experiences. He spent four years in the Goose Bay area in the late 1940s, and with a doctorate in forestry became director of the Northwestern Wildlife Station at the University of New Brunswick.

He was told that there had been numerous reports at Goose Bay and North West River of the peculiar tracks of a creature the natives knew as a "medicine bear" and who maintained they had never seen another creature like it. Further, they averred that it owed its origin to the spirit of some "bad" Indian.

Wright interviewed Mrs. Mary (Joseph) Michelin and asked her if she was certain it was not a bear that she had seen. She replied, "It was no bear Mr. Wright; I killed 12 bears on my husband's trap-line and I know their tracks well. I saw enough of this thing to be sure of that. I fired a shotgun at it and I heard the shot hit."[24]

Harold "Harry" G. Paddon, a Labrador trapper, logger, and mill manager, is unclear as to the date of this account, but it is doubtless the same as that recorded by others. He declined to identify the principals, other than the nonspecific Uncle Joe and Aunt Mary, but they were without doubt Joseph and Mary Michelin.

Is it remotely possible that Susannah saw something like this in her book and in the woods?

One day in late summer, while the Michelin's comely daughter (presumably Susannah) was hanging out the wash, she felt as if she was being watched. Certainly not high-strung, she nevertheless watched for movement in the thick brush surrounding the house. Sudden motion caught her eye, and she had a glimpse of a large hairy creature, which she was certain was not a bear. Slowly, she backed toward the house and as she did so there emerged from the thicket a huge manlike apparition, which she estimated to be more than two metres in height, even in its semi-crouch. Long, heavily-muscled arms and a grinning face lent to it the appearance of a gorilla, which Susannah had once seen in a book. As it advanced, she cried out, turned, and ran for the door.

Hearing a noise, her mother glanced out the window and instantly sized up the situation; she grabbed her shotgun and flung the door open. With her daughter in the line of fire, she was obliged to loose one barrel into the air, thereby causing the creature to pause and giving her enough of a gap to fire the second charge directly at it. Though the range was great and the load only bird-shot, it was enough to send the unwelcome caller on its way. The women said the loud cry it emitted as it took its leave was similar to the steam whistles of the lumber company's tugboats, the *Ethel* and the *Jean*.

The visitor seemed interested in the girl. She and her mother saw it often in the ensuing months; the husband and sons, however, who always went armed, never did get a look at it. Frequently, when the women were home alone, the ape-man peered in at the windows but vanished in a flash if one of them reached for a gun.

On several occasions, the creature's huge and human-like tracks were found in the hard-packed clay of the riverbank, the impressions indicative of great weight. It always approached the house from downwind, and though they growled and bristled, the dogs feared it too much to take to its trail. Moreover, they were seldom aware of its presence in time to give worthwhile warning.

As fall approached, the apparent voyeur visited nearly every night when the men were not at home. Always wary, it seemed to know where potential enemies lay in wait; the strongest bear traps had been set out, but it easily avoided them. The residents were almost certain this would end when the snow fell and they could follow its tracks.

Eight kilometres downstream was the settlement of Traverspine, larger and built around Alfred Dickie's Grand River Pulp and Paper Company. The mill, its two tugs, and 70 men were managed by George Marshall, a cross-grained and very capable Nova Scotian, whose first reaction was to ridicule the idea of this fearsome ape-creature. However, as the tales proliferated, he began to wonder. Then one day he saw the tracks for himself and was convinced enough to join in the attempts to capture the thing. On several occasions, he brought his entire force of men, armed with rifles, to lie in wait all night. During these vigils the creature stayed out of sight, but when they stopped it resumed its surveillance of the family.

In the fall, the beast's visits grew less frequent, and the Michelins speculated that it might hibernate as a bear would. After winter struck in earnest, it came no more, but over the next 30-odd years there were occasional reports of its tracks being seen.[25]

Keep in mind that these events occurred early in the last century, long before the onset of the sasquatch furor along Canada's Pacific coast and in the northwestern United States. Sightings in such a context argue toward a higher degree of truth and are, likewise, of greater potential value.[26]

No further sightings have been recorded, and the matter remains a mystery, but for one simple explanation – a hoax. In light of the strong testimony mentioned above, such an explanation might not be good enough.

All the same, according to Dr. Kester Brown, who worked with Dr. Anthony "Tony" Paddon, son of Harry Paddon, at North West River and again on the *Maraval* in 1959, the so-called Traverspine Gorilla was a practical joke. It seems that when one of the perpetrators was approaching death, he told Dr. Paddon of his part in the caper.

Decades earlier, he and a friend had been working at a lumber camp in the

Surgeon Lt. Anthony W. Paddon, RCNVR, later Dr. Tony Paddon and Governor General of Newfoundland.

vicinity of Mud Lake. One day, left behind as caretakers, they came up with a marvellous prank. The two produced a trail of huge footprints in the snow, having them appear to enter camp and engage in a scuffle with someone or something; then they dripped some blood about as proof of a massacre and had the tracks leave camp.

The jokers hid until the other men returned to discover the scene of what appeared to be a grisly encounter. The crew left in such a hurry that an explanation was impossible, and thus began the career of the Traverspine "devil." Afterward, neither man had the courage to admit that it was a joke. Paddon apparently told this story to Brown while they were on the *Maraval*, en route to Hebron in 1959.

Brown, who had since moved to Australia, said he had no idea that the tale would become part of Labrador folklore until he returned there in 1998. He marvelled that Paddon had not mentioned the event in his memoirs, rather than appearing to enforce the story. He did not think Paddon had forgotten and wondered if he thought the tale should be perpetuated.[27]

If Brown's tale is true, the anonymous jokers were dealing with remarkably stupid Labrador woodsmen and trappers. Scarcely a Boy Scout alive would be duped by tracks so easily followed in the snow and which would, eventually, lead directly to the culprits. The problems faced in leaving a convincing trail under those conditions would be insurmountable. Considering the men with whom they were dealing – all hunters and trappers – the jokers would have been lucky to escape with their lives.

Sasquatch-type beings have been said to utter uncommon and at times human-sounding cries. Perhaps this could explain Savage Cove's devil-in-residence. Nearly everyone in the vicinity of Sandwich Bay, particularly in the area of the Paradise River, has heard of it. Over the decades the noises have remained virtually unchanged; though many have searched for the cause, none have met with success. No matter how far the searchers travelled, the source always seemed to maintain a constant distance from them.

Forward Learning of Paradise River told of hearing a horrible racket at Savage Cove in the early 1900s, and he knew of others who had heard the same thing. Though he had searched for the source of the noise, he had never found it and could think of no reasonable explanation for the noises, similar to that of dogs growling and fighting and which degenerated into the sounds of people crying, screaming, and even choking.

Once, while in his early twenties and with the rashness of youth, he had taken his rifle and flashlight and gone up the hill from which the sounds seemed to emanate. When he reached the suspected area, there was only an ominous silence. Turning his light off, he stood and listened, then called out as loudly as he could in the direction from which he thought the noise may have come – not a sound. He believed that late spring and early fall were probably the best times to hear the uproar, and he was certain that whatever made them was still around the cove.[28]

In the 1920s, Ellen Learning, at nearby Calloway's Cove, heard the sounds on a calm summer evening. The human-like cries convinced her that a boat had gone ashore and the victims were in desperate straits. However, the sounds changed to those of a fight, then weeping, and finally, to that of squalling babies. Even after the bloodcurdling clamour stopped, fear kept her awake all night. Her father, a woodcutter for the Hudson Bay Company, had heard the same noises for years and said it had set his teeth on edge and the dogs to howling through the dark hours. Donald Martin, Roland McDonald, and Butler Martin camped there one summer and the fearsome cacophony often led to sleepless nights. Greatly annoyed, the audacious Don Martin went in search of the disturbance, but he, too, found nothing.

Neil Lethbridge and a partner visited the cove one September by motor boat. On a dark night, Lethbridge had taken their punt and gone ashore for water. There was no wind, but he suddenly heard "this god-awful noise." Convincing himself that it was only a bird or animal, he got his water and hastened back to the boat. The sounds were, at times, like that of an infant wailing and wolves howling, followed by appalling screeching.[29]

Margaret Davis of Happy Valley-Goose Bay told the late Doris Saunders (inspired founding editor of *Them Days* magazine) of hearing the Savage Cove Devil. She had heard others speak of the noises, and apparently the events had been numerous and recent. She asserted that it was awful, as it echoed through the hills and cliffs. The explanation she had been given was that someone was once murdered there and it was likely the victim's ghost crying out for justice or vengeance.

Some, Max Pardy among them, had heard the horrible din and afterward diligently avoided the place. Most were disbelievers until they visited the cove and heard it for themselves. While many said it was the wind blowing through the trees and around oddly shaped rocks, others were certain it was the souls of white settlers killed there years earlier by natives. The closest to a plausible, natural explanation – that the sounds could have been caused by the movement of a tree lifting sod on a stream bank when the wind blew – does not really hold water either, as the sounds were louder than ever on calm nights.[30]

This next tale connected to our mysterious forest dwellers took place some years later and was related by Thorwald Perrault of Happy Valley. He told of an odd experience that he and Albert Mitchell had while working a trap-line one October around 1930. They proposed using Uncle John Andersen's cabin at Stag Bay, about 40 kilometres southeast of Makkovik. By the time they reached it, they had accumulated a fine bag of wild fowl – 52 birds in all.

The little cabin was set back in the protection of a few wind-barbered trees and behind it was marshy ground; all around, close by, was tall grass littered with branches and twigs.

Perrault said it was all but impossible to walk about without making a noise; even a squirrel running by would be heard. The door of the shack was only about 150 centimetres high, and the bottom of its modest window was even with the top of the door. Here, throwing their blankets on the big bunk in one corner, they spent a comfortable night.

Next day, they set out a dozen or so traps and bagged an additional six partridge and a goose. They had set out their earlier bag on a large log, and after cleaning their latest catch, they hung all of them up three metres in a pair of trees standing beside the cabin. There would be no shortage of food for a while.

Shortly after supper, at the end of another long and strenuous day, they climbed into their bunk and snuffed the lantern. Around ten o'clock they were still talking when they were startled by a loud rapping on the wall above the door. The four knocks seemed to come from head height, which would suggest a tall man was standing just outside.

In unison they called out, but instead of a reply there came another four thunderous knocks that shook the walls. Immediately, there followed a tugging at the door, which had been fastened with a piece of chain from a fox trap; now it began to show the strain of a powerful pull.

Perrault picked up his .44 Winchester rifle, handed Mitchell his .30-30, then quietly approached the door. After a moment's silent wait, they threw the door open and quickly stepped out and to one side – there was nothing there. Perrault circled the cabin and met Mitchell coming around from the other direction. They had seen nothing whatever.

Returning to their bed, they discussed the heavy pounding on the door and the considerable stress exerted on the chain. They agreed that if the knocks came again they would call "Come in" once, and if there was no response they would shoot through the door. They heard nothing further and, at last, fell asleep.

At daybreak, they visited the beach but found no tracks there other than their own, and after a short inspection headed back for breakfast. As they approached the cabin, it dawned on them that their birds were gone. Those that had been in the trees had not been pulled down, but unhooked without breaking any branches. Mitchell's goose, which he had hung in a tall tree by a string around its neck, was missing a leg, and there was a pile of feathers on the ground beneath it. To Perrault it looked as if the leg had been cut off with a sharp axe.

That day they searched the woods and beach for any sign of the thief or their birds but had no luck. When night came they set traps all around the cabin, but the next morning none had been tripped or otherwise disturbed. After keeping a keen lookout for a couple of days, and still finding no sign of anything unusual, they returned home, baffled. Whatever had been there was big, could carry a substantial number of birds, and could move very quietly. They told old-timers of the event, and they were equally puzzled.[31]

Researcher Dr. Michael Taft, head of the Archive of Folk Culture at the Library of Congress in Washington, published an article called "Sasquatch-like Creatures in Newfoundland." In it he included another story, this one taken from Memorial University's Folklore and Language Archive and supposed to have taken place in the 1930s.

An uncorroborated tale is told of a Battle Point bootlegger who buried his illicit merchandise in his garden, much to the disgust of the police who never found anything. One dark night he went out to get a bottle and, after pacing off the distance, began to dig. As he did so he was startled by a light so bright that he had difficulty looking at it. The light approached, dimming as it came, and to his astonishment and terror he saw it was emitted by the huge eyes of a creature about two metres tall, covered with short, black hair.

The man, naturally, had stopped digging, and the monster

backed away slowly, its eyes dimming as the distance increased. When it had vanished into the darkness, the distraught bootlegger (his dread of this apparition more than equalling his dread of the police) hastily filled the hole and raced for his house.

Next evening, he ventured up into the garden once more. Locating the spot again, he nervously began to dig and instantly the light reappeared and approached him. He saw with relief that when he stopped digging the frightful creature moved away and its eyes dimmed. Unable to continue his work, he went back to his house to think things over. It is said that he shortly gave up his calling for something less remunerative but also less stressful.

Local folklore maintained that the creature had been set to guard a treasure hidden by pirates who had never returned. Where this may have occurred is not known, and Taft himself admitted the name he used for the settlement is false.[32] The yarn is reminiscent of more recent reports of hairy humanoids connected, in some way, with UFOs but are probably not relevant to our discussion here. The light-emitting eyes are particularly puzzling and – if we may say so – far-fetched.

In 1947, stories of Labrador "ape-men" were casually told by Dr. and Mrs. C. Hogarth Forsyth while they were in New York City raising funds for the Grenfell Association. They spent the winter there and were interviewed on January 3 by the Associated Press for its syndicated series *The March of Science*.

The interview began with details of the medical situations the Forsyths had encountered while working with Grenfell, but during the second half the subject of Labrador ape-men came up. They explained that when they first arrived they had laughed off such tales as legends, but over the next few years they had found the locals to be very literal minded and not much given to myths. The stories were based on many accounts of giant barefoot tracks in the snow, usually found by trappers whose living depended on their knowledge of such things. Often they traced the tracks to "nests," which were usually beneath protective trees and hidden by surrounding brush. A newspaper column stated the following in support of the ape-men's cunning: "The trail usually runs out on glare ice or in running water. But such trails have been followed as much as twenty-five kilometres over rough country. Whatever made them climbed easily over stumps and other obstructions where an ordinary man would have gone around; and whatever it was, it walked on two feet."[33]

The sightings were likely within 400 kilometres of Cartwright, since that was the centre of Forsyth's operations. There being no roads, transportation was mostly by water, and there was little travel in the interior. During their 15 years in Labrador, the Forsyths heard only two reports of people who had actually caught glimpses of the ape-men, and it is unclear if the incidents occurred before or during their stay (1932–1946).[34]

The Gulf Coast Bigfoot Research Organization – a leader in the search for answers to the mysterious ape-man question – collects reports worldwide and recently added two more accounts from Newfoundland and Labrador.

The first came from a resident of Labrador, in all likelihood an Innu, who repeated a tale he had heard from the "old people," of an event that took place on the trap-line. On a frosty morning in the 1950s, three trappers were walking on a frozen and snow-covered lake when a sudden movement caught their eye. There, on the shore, was what appeared to be a huge hairy man hunkered down with its back to them, picking among the willow roots.

The astounded men stopped in their tracks and one tentatively lifted his rifle. As he did so, the creature became aware of their presence and turned to face them. The man who told the story said a curious compassion crept over him, and he grasped the other's rifle, pushing it out of line. The creature turned and glancing back over its shoulder walked into the woods and vanished from sight.

All three acknowledged being frightened, and as often happens, they told no one of their encounter. For years they kept their silence, but when similar stories cropped up in books, newspapers, and on television, they came forward. However, even today the two surviving trappers seldom mention it; those they have told, however, are now believers. The person who informed the GCBRO of the occurrence said that, while he had never seen such a thing, he and others firmly believed that the elder recounted an event that had happened exactly as described.[35]

The second incident occurred on St. John Island, which is about 15 kilometres north of Port au Choix and seven offshore. Around 1965, some families were camping there when at dusk two little girls visited the privy, a hundred metres from the campfire where the others had congregated. They heard something cautiously moving about outside but paid little attention. As they were about to leave, the eldest spied, through a gap at the bottom of the door, a pair of huge feet covered with coarse black hair. Opening the door a crack, she was confronted by a colossal and equally hairy ogre. Whimpering, she slammed the door; the younger girl began

Many were certain that such a creature did not exist, but the Innu knew better.

146

to cry, prompting the first to do so as well. Far from their parents, they were understandably frightened.

The prowler moved around to the back of the outhouse, and the girls took this opportunity to make a dash for the campfire. The others were all there; no one was near the outhouse, no other humans were on the island, and there were no bears in the region. Admittedly, many things look huge to a four-year-old, but this was something completely unfamiliar. The storyteller explained that she would have been less sure of her experience had her mother not prompted the memory of it when she was a teenager.[36]

A more recent and more amusing "Newfoundland bigfoot" event occurred on the evening of December 11, 2005. A Florida man reported seeing a sasquatch-like creature on his property when leaving for work. As he headed down his driveway toward the road, an enormous black animal caught his attention. Snatching up his camera, he managed to make a single exposure before the menace disappeared in the brush near the lakeshore. He estimated it to be nearly two metres long and a metre-and-a-half tall. He had no idea what it was, but suspected it might have been an escaped gorilla. He later announced the identification of his mystery visitor. As was the case in Devon, it turned out to be a neighbour's Newfoundland dog, this time from across the lake, who had been out for an early morning swim and stroll. One sympathetic soul who had suspected as much after seeing the photo, facetiously suggested it might be a gorilla in a dog suit. In the meantime, there have been some reports of these strange creatures seen in Trinity Bay, but more detailed or more interesting information has not been found.

Many of these sightings are hard to explain away. A dog may figure in the incident noted above, but certainly not in all of them. It will be no surprise to cat-lovers that cats also figure in some very strange incidents throughout the province. We'll turn to those mysterious felines next.

1. Alan Baker, *The Encyclopedia of Alien Encounters* (London: Virgin Publishing Ltd., 1999), 35.

2. George M. Eberhart, *Mysterious Creatures: A Guide to Cryptozoology* (Santa Barbara, CA: ABC-CLIO, 2002), 223–25.

3. John Bindernagel, *North America's Great Ape: The SASQUATCH* (Courtenay, BC: Beachcomber Books, 2008).

4. Dawn Prince-Hughes, *The Archetype of the Ape-man: The Phenomenological Archaeology of a Relic Hominid Ancestor*, Dissertation.com, USA (1997), 66.

5. Carol Rose, *Giants, Monsters, and Dragons: An Encyclopedia of Folklore, Legend, and Myth* (Santa Barbara, CA: ABC-CLIO, 2000), 67, 363.

6. Ernest William Hawkes, "The Labrador Eskimo," *Memoirs of the Canada Department of Mines Geological Survey* (Ottawa: 1916), 143–50.

7. Mark A. Hall, "Homo gardarensis – A Different Kind of Bigfoot," *Wonders*, 5, no. 1 (March 1998), 3–32.

8. Joshua Obed and& Kako Kajuaitsiak, "Inuit Legends," *Them Days*, 10, no. 1 (Happy Valley-Goose Bay, NL, September, 1984), 16–21.

9. A. M. Reeves, N. L. Beamish & R. B. Anderson, "Saga of Eric the Red," *The Norse Discovery of America* (Stockholm: Norrœna Society, 1906), 55.

10. Dale Mackenzie Brown, "The Fate of Greenland's Vikings," *Archaeology*, Archaeological Institute of America (2000), www.archaeology.org/online/features/greenland

11. Einar Haugen Thompson, *Voyages to Vinland* (New York: Alfred A. Knopf, 1942), 144.

12. Prince-Hughes, *The Archetype of the Ape-man*, 66.

13. Thomas Wentworth Higginson, "The Island of Demons," *Tales of the Enchanted Islands of the Atlantic* (Amsterdam: Fredonia Books, 2001), 205–19.

14. James P. Howley, FGS., *The Beothucks or Red Indians: The Aboriginal Inhabitants of Newfoundland* (Cambridge: Cambridge University Press, 1915), 247.

15. Michael Taft, "Sasquatch-like Creatures in Newfoundland: A Study in the Problems of Belief, Perception and Reportage," in *Manlike Monsters on Trial*, eds. Marjorie Alpin & Michael Ames,(Vancouver: University of British Columbia Press, 1980), 90.

16. John T. Rowland, *North to Adventure* (New York: W. W. Norton & Co., 1963), 93–94.

17. E. C. Robinson, FGS., *In An Unknown Land* (London: Elliot Stock, 1909), 134–38.

148

18. Lionel Leslie, *Wilderness Trails in Three Continents: An Account of Travel, Big Game Hunting and Exploration in India, Burma, China, East Africa and Labrador* (London: Heath Cranton, 1931), 197–98.

19. Ibid.

20. Dawn E. Bastian & Judy K. Mitchell, *Handbook of Native American Mythology* (Oxford: ABC-CLIO, 2004), 223–24.

21. Elliott Merrick, *True North* (New York: Charles Scribner & Sons, 1933), 24–26.

22. Harry Paddon, *The Labrador Memoir of Dr. Harry Paddon, 1912–1938.* ed. Ronald Rompkey (Montreal: McGill-Queen's University Press, 2003), 92.

23. Philip H. Godsell, "Ask Adventure (column)," *Adventure Magazine*, Popular Publications, New York, NY.

24. Bruce S. Wright, *Wildlife Sketches: Near and Far* (Fredericton, NB: Brunswick Press, 1962), 253–54.

25. Harold G. Paddon, *Green Woods and Blue Waters*, (St. John's, NL: Breakwater Books Ltd., 1989), 117–21.

26. Gary A. Mangiacopra & Dwight G. Smith, "Canada's Headless Valley Revisited," *North American BioFortean Review*, 8, no. 1, issue 18 (January 2006), 8–10.

27. Kester A. M. Brown, "Myth Exploded or Another Tall Tale," *Them Days*, 23, no. 4, (Summer, 1998), 44.

28. Forward Learning, "Savage Cove Devil," *Them Days*, 2, no. 2, (December 1976), 28.

29. Lynne D. Fitzhugh, *The Labradorians: Voices from the Land of Cain* (St. John's, NL: Breakwater Books Ltd., 1999), 188–90.

30. Ibid.

31. Thorward Perrault, "Mystery Unsolved," *Them Days* (June 1977), 32–35.

32. Marjorie Halpin & Michael M. Ames, eds, *Manlike Monsters on Trial: Early Records and Modern Evidence* (Vancouver: University of British Columbia Press, 1987), 87–88; & Matthew Krucak, "Something Big Afoot," *The Telegram* (St. John's), February 2, 2008, F30.

33. "Giant Barefoot Tracks in Labrador Snows Give Hint of Mystery Race of 'Ape-Men,'" *The Morning Journal* (Daytona Beach, FL), January 6, 1947, 6.

34. Ibid.

35. "From the Files of (G.C.B.R.O.)" Gulf Coast Bigfoot Research Organization, accessed March 16, 2010, http://www.gcbro.com/CAnf002.html.

36. Ibid.

chapter

six

ALIEN BI*g* CATS

"ALIEN BIG CATS" (or "ABCs") is the term now being applied to felines found far from their natural habitats: "alien" meaning out of place rather than extraterrestrial. These animals, chiefly leopards, panthers, and cougars, have apparently been seen worldwide and at great distances from their conventional homes. Surprisingly, wilderness-free Great Britain seems to be infested with them, and reports have come from more than 30 counties.

In the folklore of Scotland, and to a lesser degree that of Ireland, the *Cait Sith* or *Cat Sídhe*, a big black cat with a white spot on its chest, is legendary. This phantasmal feline haunts the Scottish Highlands. Some stories suggest the *Cait Sith*, or "fairy cat," is a transformed witch.

Dr. Shuker suggests in *Mystery Cats of the World* that the legends were inspired by what are known as "Kellas cats," named for the village of Kellas where they were first recorded, likely a hybrid of domestic varieties and European wildcats. Today these large, black wildcats, with some features of domestic cats, are found exclusively in Scotland and have existed there for possibly two millennia or more.

The Scottish wildcat – antecedent of the mysterious Cait Sith?

The cats being reported today are more substantial, but the Kellas cat theory has been largely ignored. Most of the numerous photographs that have been taken are fuzzy and indistinct, leading skeptics to suggest that large house cats or farm cats are being mistaken for ABCs. Nevertheless, additional evidence in the form of grisly sheep and calf carcasses has been discovered in farmers' fields: many carcasses stripped of their flesh and with claw marks on their necks and bellies indicating that they were not victims of the area's usual predators. In September 1993, the remains of sheep were discovered in Whorlton, County Durham, where peculiar-looking feces were also found not far from the site. These were analysed by the famous South African zoologist Dr. Hans Kruuk of the Institute of Terrestrial Ecology at Aberdeen. He acknowledged, "My examinations all point to a puma (*Puma concolor*) or a leopard (*Panthera pardus*), but since no sightings exist in Durham of a spotted creature my conclusions would favour a puma."[1]

As if to dispute this claim, Paul Sieveking, writing in *Fortean Times*, said that at least four Asian leopards (*Felis bengalensis*) have been shot or found dead in Britain in the past dozen or so years. However, unidentified big cats have been seen on the Isle of Wight for more than a hundred years with more than 300-odd sightings reported there in the past 15 years alone.[2]

152

For the most part, the cats have confined their predations to farm animals and pets, although there have been documented attacks on humans. In December 1993, Nick and Sally Dyke of Stourbridge in England's West Midlands were searching for the so-called Beast of Inkberrow, a big cat reported to be at large in the county of Hereford and Worcester, when they found more than they had bargained for. The couple boldly baited a path with dead chickens; upon returning to see if they had been successful, Nick literally stumbled over a huge black cat feeding on chicken in the grass of St. Peter's churchyard. It turned abruptly, bowling him over, then charged at Sally, knocking her down with a single swipe of its paw. Its claws penetrated her several layers of clothing, leaving three 13-centimetre-long wounds in her side. The Dykes did not tell anyone of the incident at the time as Sally, a teacher of veterinary medicine, cleaned her own wounds and took antibiotics to prevent infection.[3] Who would have believed them if they had told?

Perhaps the most famous of the ABCs is the legendary Beast of Bodmin, which is said to haunt the moorlands around that area of Cornwall. Though it had been seen on numerous occasions, it was not until December 1993 that it was videotaped by Rosemary Rhodes of Ninestones Farm. She stopped keeping sheep after four of her ewes were ripped to pieces by some animal. Her video showed what appeared to be a black leopard or panther.[4]

Some have suggested the cats are descended from animals that have escaped from zoos and private collections of exotic creatures, while others have put forward the intriguing, but perhaps unprovable, theory that the animals have stumbled into space warps (portals to parallel universes?) and have been teleported from one location (their natural habitat) to another (the British countryside).

It is interesting to note that tales of similar animals have come from Afghanistan, via members of our Canadian military

The black variety of cat is not a different species, as is evidenced by this magnificent jaguar, but is a result of melanosis.

and CNN News. In August 2003, a large unknown predator was said to have killed a number of people north of Kabul. The beast exhibited both canine and feline traits, and was likened to everything from a tiger to a fox. Some Afghans of the region were certain it was a creature brought in by the United States' government for villainous intent, but this was categorically denied by army spokesman Colonel Roger Davis.[5]

The cougar's names are as varied as its geographical habitats. It is known as a mountain lion, panther, catamount, king cat, and puma, among others. They range from the Yukon in the north to Tierra del Fuego on the southern tip of South America, all along the continental west coast and as far east as – Newfoundland? As a predator at the top of the food chain, the cougar has been persecuted unmercifully by man and driven to seek new homes even if these areas are not as suitable as its former habitat.

Unbelievably adaptable and agile, they have great leaping ability and are good climbers; although they are respectable swimmers, they prefer dry land. Their sense of smell is not great, but their sight and hearing are exceptional. Chiefly nocturnal, their activity peaks at dusk and dawn, and they must hunt over a wide area, as much as 100 square kilometres by some estimates.

The last confirmed case of a cougar in eastern North America was one trapped in Maine, just across the Canadian border, in 1938. However, Dr. Bruce Wright, who conducted hundreds of independent searches to find evidence of what is generally regarded as an extinct or forgotten feline, documented 220 reports from New Brunswick and 25 from Nova Scotia between 1948 and 1971. One day in 1972, while driving to investigate a reported sighting, he was startled to see what was, presumably, an eastern cougar crossing the road in front of him. This was in the "wilderness" of the Canadian Maritimes, and the event encouraged him to search for a solution to the mystery as nothing else could have.[6] Unfortunately, Wright passed away in 1975, having received little but ridicule from his colleagues. They considered it a waste of time to hunt for a mammal that the mainstream scientific community regarded as non-existent. Lacking an advocate of his calibre, his work, to a large degree, lapsed.

Stories of big cats in Newfoundland and Labrador were rather meagre for many years – actually there were none. Someone recently pointed out that along the Labrador coast, near Drunken Harbour Tickle in the vicinity of Postville, stands a

Our native lynx, a rare find in the forests of the province today.

prominence that has been known by the name "Panther Hill" for decades. It might appear obvious that it was named to commemorate the sighting of some sort of big cat there. Not quite.

Leonard McNeill explained that it was called Panther Hill because in the early 1900s his grandmother took advantage of its summit to watch for her husband's schooner returning from Turnavik. The schooner's name? *Panther.*[7]

There is, however, a Mountain Cat Lake in Labrador, named for the mountain cat, whatever that might be. In *A Woman's Way through Unknown Labrador*, Mina Hubbard wrote that the lake was a "gem in its setting of hills."[8] One authority suggested that Hubbard may have named it so because of its shape – she had a proclivity for calling geographical features for whatever they reminded her of – but a close examination of the lake reveals no resemblance to a cat of any sort. Bryan Greene, co-editor of *The Woman Who Mapped Labrador: The Life and Expedition Diary of Mina Hubbard*, contends that the term "mountain cat" was used by trappers in referring to the pine marten, but no substantiation of such usage has been found.[9] Furthermore, there is a Mountain Cat Point on the south side of The Backway, the easternmost end of Lake Melville, whose name has yet to be explained.

According to conventional science, Newfoundland and Labrador has but one big cat: the lynx, of which we have two subspecies. Those common to Labrador are *Lynx canadensis*, while those on the island of Newfoundland are *Lynx subsolanus*. At one time both were plentiful, but the predations of man and his destruction of their habitat have reduced them to a rarity. In any case, a lynx bears very little resemblance to a cougar.

At about a metre in length and weighing 10 to 12 kilograms, the lynx vaguely looks like a very large, furry house cat. In summer, it is reddish brown, but in winter it turns a light

The cougar is an impressive and accomplished predator.

grey with dark spots. To complement its stubby black-tipped tail and tufted ears, it also has a beard-like ruff and large furry feet.

The cougar is much larger. A big male can weigh up to 100 kilograms and its length can approach two-and-a-half metres from nose to tail tip, though most are usually much smaller. This powerful brute has a relatively small broad head with little rounded ears, a muscular body, long hind legs, and a long tail tipped with black. Its colour varies from slate grey, through

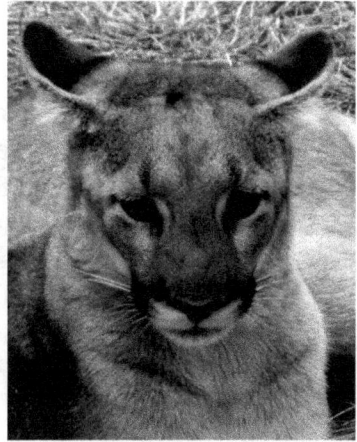

yellow buff, to light reddish brown. "Black panther" is commonly used in connection with large black cats, but it does not refer to a distinct species; it is a colour variant caused by a particularly high concentration of the dark-brown to black pigment, melanin, that occurs naturally in the skin and hair. Oddly enough, reports from around the world frequently equate the size of these big cats as bigger than a Labrador retriever, which puts them at about one-half the size of a cougar or even less.

Size or colour were not mentioned when, around 1993–94, some residents in the region of Eastport, Happy Adventure, and Sandy Cove told of fleeting glimpses of a large cat much like a cougar in the woods near the built-up areas. The incidents made the newspapers, and there was much conjecture; however, without further appearances to fuel speculation the incidents faded from public memory.

Then, in 1998, *The Times Globe* of St. John, New Brunswick, reported that the Canadian Wildlife Service receives between 20 and 25 calls regarding big cats from residents of New Brunswick, Nova Scotia, and Newfoundland and Labrador each year. It also emphasized that the organization has yet to discover any concrete evidence that cougars are calling these regions home.[10]

Nonetheless, during the summer of 1999, some strange beast made an appearance at St. Phillips, on the eastern side of Conception Bay. According to Dale Jarvis (our well-known recorder of the bizarre) at about 11:00 p.m. one evening a family dog began howling and barking frantically, seemingly badly frightened by something or other. The women of the house went outside to see what the object of the dog's attention could possibly be and heard perplexing noises from the nearby woods. After peering into the darkness without discovering the cause, she called her husband who, being an inventive fellow and hoping to see what his wife had not, drove his pickup truck into the backyard. In the glare of its headlights he saw green-glowing eyes in the brush. Though obscured by darkness and bushes, whatever was there was obviously very big and very black. The couple and their son caught a glimpse of a large animal as it glided effortlessly through the woods to disappear into the night. Afterward, the three agreed it seemed to be sort of half-dog, half-cat.

Another episode followed in September, also at St. Phillips. This time the informant was aroused at 5:00 a.m., again by an agitated dog, and upon going outside was astonished to see what resembled a wolf in his yard staring straight at him; it was a beautiful animal, big, jet-black, and powerful-looking. Calling his dog inside he closed the door and put food down to quiet it, then checked again. He found his visitor had gone.[11]

Though it is doubtful that such an unlikely new hybrid has evolved unbeknownst to science, these accounts arouse curiosity. Recall the half-canine, half-feline of Afghanistan. If these creatures, improbable as they are, do not constitute a mystery, it is certainly a good approximation of one.

Newfoundland's next known experience with a possible alien big cat took place in early August 2000. Chris Moss, a St. John's student employed as coordinator of the Eastport Peninsula's *Celebration 2000*, had made his weekly trip home. Upon his return to work on Monday morning, he asked an acquaintance what he knew of wild cats on the island. Given a brief description of Newfoundland's lynx, Moss elaborated; around dusk the previous evening, not far west of Clarenville and while driving into the setting sun, he was surprised when a large cat leapt across the road just 100 or so metres away. Although he saw it only in silhouette, he knew that it was definitely a cat but one larger than a Newfoundland dog, lean, and with a long tail. He was understandably reluctant to share that he had seen such an animal.[12]

The next occurrence found in local lore took place a few years ago when Harold Pritchett of Gander was tending his rabbit snares between the highway and Gander Lake. He took a moment to admire the sky and water, and he, too, was caught unawares when a large black cat with a long tail casually strolled into view and then disappeared among the alders.

Some time passed without any cats whatsoever frightening the bejesus out of residents. Finally, in June 2005, further evidence of something unusual came along. Gord Lee took his Rottweiler for a walk along the woodland track known as Pond Road, only metres from his home at the western extremity of Happy Adventure. The two had not ambled far up the hill when they came face to face with a large cat sitting placidly in the middle of the trail grooming itself. They watched it for a moment before the cat took notice of them. After inspecting the man and dog for a few seconds, it got to its feet, elegantly slid into the woods, and disappeared.

A woodsman of some wide experience – both in this province and around the country – Lee knew exactly what he had seen. He contacted a friend, well-known photojournalist Lynn Ball who has a summer home in Salvage, and they returned to the spot, where they photographed the tracks.

Biologist John Gosse of Terra Nova National Park heard of the event and called on Lee at his home. Lee told Goss that the first thing apparent to him was the long tail extending up and over the animal's back, ending in a "crook" at the top; it reminded him of a monkey! He further described the cat as about a metre long, a half-metre in height, and weighing about 35 kilograms. If it had been a cougar, it must have been an immature one, but Lee added that at a distance of about 20 metres it was still difficult to judge.

Lee presented Gosse with a picture of a track in the mud, and though it was rather indefinite, the experts confirmed that if it was not a cougar track it was something very like one. What, on this island, could have possibly produced a track similar to that of a cougar? After hearing of the encounter, a

Tracks left by a cougar's forefeet are usually nine to ten centimetres across and show no claw marks.

These tracks, found near Happy Adventure, appear to be even larger than most when compared to the sunglasses beside them, perhaps as much as 12 centimetres across.

resident of neighbouring Glovertown admitted to being thankful that someone else had reported seeing a cougar in such an unlikely place. Evidently, he had chanced upon the same or a similar beast but was reluctant to tell anyone and be regarded as a crackpot. Lee had also heard of a similar sighting in the area around Gambo Pond at about that time.

On June 8, 2010, Gosse talked with Mrs. Morgan of Sandy Cove. She and her husband, Dr. Arthur Morgan, twice had an uncommon visitor: once in early October 2009 and again in May 2010. Each time, a large black cat passed through their back yard; on the last occasion, it jumped three or four metres up a tree in a single bound. She described it as being certainly larger than a house cat, with a long tail with a "loop" at the end, black with a faint tawny streak. She was somewhat concerned for her safety, as she spends much time in the garden.

Gosse also spoke with the Morgan's neighbours, Gail and Terry King, who told him they had seen a large black cat-like animal cross the road between Eastport and Sandringham, near the Sutreen Hardwoods plant. At a distance they thought it was a bear cub, but upon approaching it they noticed the tail. Since there were no photographs and no physical evidence from these two cases, Gosse set up a video camera on the Morgan's property and left if for about a week. It captured many photos, mostly of Dr. Morgan working in his garden, and one of an inquisitive black bear.

On July 13 at the Park's Visitors Centre, Gosse spoke to a couple from St. John's, who said they had seen what they thought to be a cougar on top of Ochre Hill back in the early 1990s. The woman described it as much bigger than a domestic cat, brown, having a long looping tail, and moving like a cat. The man said he had photographed it and would look for the picture, but nothing has been forthcoming.[13]

Most convincing was Eric Nippard of Springdale who told of an experience he had in 2006. He and two friends were driving along Salmon Pond Road, presumably near his home town (there is a better known Salmon Pond Road a few kilometres west of Glenwood), when a big cat crossed in front of them. Nippard said it walked calmly, not even bothering to turn its head to look at the truck. It was only about 25 metres from them and "was a cougar type of cat with a square nose." He estimated its weight at 25 kilograms or more, not large for a cougar but it certainly would have been an enormous house cat. Though he had a camera in the vehicle, he was, understandably, so surprised that he did not even think of getting it out in the few seconds he had. "I was amazed when I saw it," said Nippard. "If it's a rumour, it's not a rumour in my book. I saw it as clear as day. It was completely black, no other colour on it anywhere."[14]

He passed the information on to authorities a few days later but heard nothing in response. "I was feeling a little put out," he said. "You wonder if people believe you. We did see it, it was here, but I haven't seen it since."[15]

He asked around, and one of those he questioned told him a story of American sportsmen who had brought four big cats to the Great Northern Peninsula in the 1960s to provide an exciting hunt. Luckily, for at least two of the cats, a snowstorm came up and they escaped from the simple-minded criminals.[16] It is difficult to say if there is any truth to this.

Another story of the cats' origin came from a caller to Bill Rowe's talk show on VOCM, a local radio station. He told of two steel cages having been found in the woods near Stephenville sometime between 1950 and 1955. It was rumoured these cages had contained wolves or cougars, and while this too is perhaps an urban legend, it should not be completely discounted.[17]

On October 1, 2006, the provincial Department of Natural Resources acknowledged that reports of large cats, specifically large black cats, had increased. Though they had checked into the stories that had come from all over the Green Bay area, they had little luck in finding hard evidence.[18]

One such report from the region between Halls Bay and Green Bay was made by jogger Wade Pynn, who was startled by a large black cat with a long tail on Tuesday, September 30, 2008. Pynn reported his discovery to the police and, again, the news item was carried by VOCM. On October 1, it stated:

> It's not the kind of thing you hear about every day in this province. Springdale RCMP have notified provincial wildlife officials after a number of reports in the last two to three weeks about a large black cat or black panther-like animal with a long tail in the woods in the Springdale/ Green Bay area. Constable Danny Williams says a couple of people claim to have seen it and they've had numerous people asking them about it. Williams says people should be on the lookout for the creature.[19]

Soon after, there appeared in the *Nor'wester*, a similar write-up headed "Big Cat Concerns Prompt Official Reaction."[20]

These accounts motivated a man identified only as Terry to call Linda Swain's VOCM radio talk show. He claimed to have seen such an animal six years earlier, playing at cat-and-mouse with a fox in the 35-kilometre stretch of terrain between Roddickton and Main Brook. He and a companion had been hunting moose when they happened upon the scene of the unusual skirmish. Fascinated, they watched the action through binoculars for roughly three minutes from a distance of some 300 metres.

It was at about that time a rumour began to circulate to the effect that a cat had escaped from the *Fabuleux Cirque Estival*, a circus which had visited the area the previous summer. On November 6, the *Nor'wester* ran an article under the headline, "Truth to Feline Rumours? Circus Says No Missing Animals." The article went on to explain that officials of the Department of Natural Resources were taking the reports seriously, and Conservation Officers Mark Lawlor and Len Pollett told of their efforts to trap the beast. One of their investigations turned up something less than a "clue." A number of residents said they had seen a black cat, but the sizes given varied from that of a large domestic cat to what may have been a cougar.

Concerns that it was the black jaguar from the *Fabuleux Cirque Estival* were soon quelled; the mere suggestion drew laughter from Louis Leonard, the manager. He declared emphatically that the valuable animal – owned by Michael Hackenberger's zoo at Bowmanville, Ontario – certainly had not gone astray during the trip.[21]

Officers attempted to follow up on reports but were stymied by the lack of physical evidence and the considerable distances between sightings. Neither could anyone provide a photo nor even point to a track, a clump of fur, or a bit of cougar scat. This is not to say that many would recognize this sort of evidence either, as there is a complete lack of knowledge in this province of the size or habits of these beasts; consider the distress the inoffensive coyote has caused.

Lawlor admitted there had been enough plausible accounts

of the cat or cats to convince them there was something out there, and he fervently hoped someone would come up with some sort of corroborative evidence.[22]

Sightings continued, and the *Nor'wester* kept everyone up-to-date. The newspaper, having asked the public to send in their stories which it promised to investigate, received numerous responses. The issue of November 22, told of a big cat that had been seen taking its ease on the deck of the Riverwood Inn, beside the Indian River on the southwest side of Springdale. Two more accounts came from those who had been startled by a big cat casually strolling along a local hiking trail. Marlene Burton of South Brook, which is less than ten kilometres south of Springdale at the bottom of Halls Bay, said she had seen one there. It is not even remotely possible that the widely scattered stories could have been caused by one cat, even a very fast one.

Ed Smith of Springdale, the well-known author, acknowledged in his province-wide column of November 8, that he had long scoffed at the idea of such animals having moved onto the island of Newfoundland. Then, one night at a bridge game, one of his friends mentioned that he had seen one of these creatures close to the tree line a few metres from his back door. Further, he said there was no doubt in the world that it was a cougar. Smith, knowing the man well, was no longer quite as skeptical and (good sport that he is) went on to apologize to those at whom he had poked fun.[23] It was well he did so; there was to be no respite.

Sharon Dove, owner of Bubbles and Bows, a dog-grooming enterprise in Springdale, brought her dogs inside when they began making a commotion on the morning of November 25. But when they continued to bark she went to the window to see what the cause might be and found they had been barking at "a little kitty cat."

She wondered if the splendid black cat on the fence might be hungry, and good-heartedly took it a can of ham flakes, though she did not want to get too close to the stranger. When she flipped the ham in its direction, the cat rose up and hissed at her, showing some large and dangerous-looking fangs. At that point she cried, "Oh, my God! It's not a little cat!"[24]

Backing into the house she grabbed her camera and took three quick photos, then phoned her husband who told her to stay inside and call the RCMP. She did so, and the police were quickly on the scene. They, in turn, called the Department of Natural Resources and soon a conservation officer was there to check things out.

As Officer Mark Lawlor had said earlier, there had been enough credible accounts for them to take the sightings seriously, and though reports varied, it was obvious people were seeing something. To complicate things, reports continued to come in from such diverse areas that investigating them all was close to impossible. As well, the size of the cat or cats varied from that of an overgrown house cat to a large cougar.

After viewing Dove's photos, officials from Corner Brook said the Department of Natural Resources acknowledged they had received several complaints of an unidentified catlike animal in the area, but did not elaborate.[25]

Nearing the end of 2008, residents around the Port au Choix Peninsula began seeing the big black cats. Aaron Beswick, of the newspaper *Northern Pen*, interviewed Marina Ploughman of the town of Port au Choix concerning her sighting of a large feline. He was told that she knew precisely what she had seen; a big black – very black – cat with a long tail.

While driving along the gravel side-road south of Hawke's Bay and near Whaleback Pond, en route to her cabin, she was stunned when the big animal crossed the road a mere 15 metres or so in front of her. She had gotten a good look at it and guessed the animal to be about a metre in length with a tail somewhat longer. She said, "It just strutted right across the road in front of me – its paws were just awesome to see spread out on the road – and its teeth – big fangs."[26]

At first she thought it was a feral cat, a domestic gone wild, but it had been much too big. Then, it occurred to her that it may have been the same animal reported in the Springdale area some weeks earlier. Her uncommon remark concerning the animal's feet splaying out on the packed gravel tends to lend more credence to her account.

Memorial University's Dr. Alistair Bath observed, "The description you have is not bad. They're about waist height and the long tail is usually a giveaway....They have muscular shoulders but curling of the tail, not so much, just at the end."

He added that the possibility of finding such a beast on the island was negligible. He thought such a creature could only have come from Quebec where there may be "only a couple of them, anyway."[27]

A diligent reporter, Beswick did a little checking and turned up a few other stories in the region between Rocky Harbour and New Ferolle, a strip of about 175 kilometres of mostly uninhabited coastline. One of those to whom he spoke was Earl Keough of Parsons Pond, a trapper and fisherman. While many old woodsmen take an obscure delight in practising upon greenhorns, Keough does not appear to be one of them.

Keough explained that he was in camp one evening with a party of hunters when they heard what they were quite certain was the scream of a big cat. He described it as sounding as though a woman was being dragged about by her hair. Regarding his own pate, he allowed, "All the hair stood up on my head." A startled hunter in the party blurted, "I didn't know you have cats – that's a cougar!" Keough then promptly named three other individuals from the area who said they had seen one of the felines.[28]

In another instance, a couple driving eastward toward Clarenville on May 7, 2010, were passing through Terra Nova National Park at around 11:30 a.m. when the usual lookout for moose was interrupted. In the ditch, along the north side of the road, a beige animal disappeared into the undergrowth. It was a drizzly day but visibility was fairly good, and though the animal was in sight for only a split second and at a distance of about 60 metres, it was obviously not a coyote and appeared too big to be a fox.[29]

Apparently, few have considered that perhaps these cats are a result of a sort of devolution or re-evolution, if you will. Could these possibly be descendants of house cats returned to the wild, as is suspected in the case of the *Kellas cats*? Is it possible that such a case of regression could have taken place over the course of only a few hundred years? There is at least as great a possibility of this being the case as there is of cats arriving from other dimensions, having gotten stuck in a space warp, or of otherwise sensible people suddenly having hallucinations en masse.

It is generally accepted that house cats have descended from cats of the wild and have likely become progressively smaller over the centuries. If these domesticated cats were returned to the wild only those best suited to that life, as per the theory of evolution, would survive and flourish.

Let us suppose that the larger cat is better equipped for survival than the smaller, and let us further suppose that the off-spring of these larger cats becomes progressively bigger with each generation. This could account for the sightings of cats midway between the size of a house cat and a cougar. In fact, the world's largest known house cat weighed in at something more than 21 kilograms. It would also explain the divergent traits with regards to colour, shape, and temperament. However, some, who seem to know what they are talking about, are firm in their belief that, unlike dogs, cats lack the genetic plasticity to breed to huge sizes. Regardless of improved diet, cats have stayed pretty much the same size since they were first domesticated: the largest breeds are generally less than ten kilograms.

There are also other less scientific factors to be considered. If you should hear of a Colin Brown, who recently hit a 120-kilogram cougar with his pickup truck north of Carmanville, pay no heed. The story continues; the owner of the nearby property

While a cougar can be big and may kill a moose, it is unlikely one has dragged such a beast around the highway near Carmanville; unless hungry, they would rather nap.

saw the same cat drag a 235-kilogram moose off into the woods. Brown's neighbour, supposedly an amateur taxidermist, planned to stuff it.

A quick check shows that this yarn pervades the Internet and is rumoured to have also taken place in Nova Scotia and in no fewer than 12 states. Besides the location, the only variable is the driver's name and the cat's victim. It actually took place in Arizona where such creatures are not rare, and the prey was a deer.

More recent reports have come to light. On January 2010, friends at a cabin heard unidentified blood-curdling screams at night. The idea that it might be a big cat did not occur to them, and they concluded only that someone had been badly injured. It took but a minute for the men to leap onto snowmobiles and roar off down the trail in the direction of the sound, one going left and the other right where the trail diverged. One had gone only a half-kilometre when he was startled by the sight of a pair of glowing eyes staring from the brush. Though familiar with eyes glowing in headlamps, he had seen none like these before.

At a distance of ten metres, he stopped and stared back for some seconds; apparently the animal thought it was well hidden, and it would have been but for the headlamps of the snowmobile. Suddenly, it burst from the trees and vanished on the other side of the trail. The brief glimpse allowed our protagonist to describe the animal as black, shiny, and big as a full-grown mountain lion – it left tracks bigger than a man's hand.

Moments later his friend showed up and called, "Follow me; you have to come see this." About 100 metres down the side-trail lay a moose, steam still rising from its torn throat. Claw marks were evident along its back and around its belly. The pair convinced themselves it had been killed by a bear and did not report it until encouraged by the following accounts.[30]

On March 30, 2011, at about 8:15 p.m., a resident of Stephenville reported seeing a huge cat "like a black panther," near Cold Brook. While he did not give his name, he insisted that he cared not a whit whether he was believed or not.

On August 15, 2011, Nelson Jackman saw a long-tailed black panther near the Hermitage dump, on the Bay d'Espoir highway, while riding his bicycle there. Taking its time, as if it was following a trail, it crossed the road then ambled up an incline into the woods. Two days later, at around 8:30 p.m., Ross Strickland ran across what he described as a "large black panther" while driving through Gros Morne National Park en route to Deer Lake.[31]

Encouraged by the fact that others had seen it, a woman identified only as Sandra reported that her male companion and her son, while hunting moose near Meadows on the north shore of the Bay of Islands in October 2007, had told of seeing a large black cat. The man was more than familiar with the area and wildlife around Monkey Pond, having hunted there for years. Upon their return they spoke of seeing a cat "the size of your dog," which weighed about 17 kilograms. She quickly dismissed it as a tall tale and commented that perhaps someone's cat had gotten loose.

However, on October 8, 2011, she had her mind changed. That day she was on her way to Corner Brook, driving down Hughes Brook hill just north of the city dump when a large black cat leapt across the road in front of her. It took but four jumps to cross the 13 metres of roadway and vanish into the woods. She thought it was about the same size as a big lynx, an animal with which she was familiar, possibly a half-metre tall, nearly a metre in length, and with a half-metre long tail. While it was solid black, it was not shiny but had a rough-textured coat. This occurred about 15 kilometres from the sighting of four years earlier. She had an excellent view of the creature and immediately called the Department of Environment and Conservation who heard her story without comment.[32]

In case you've been thinking that all has been quiet on the feline front for some time, other big cats have been reported in the intervening months, particularly along the island's west coast. Do not be lulled into complacency by an animal that depends on furtiveness to survive. Keep your eyes open when you go outside, particularly at night.

1. "Huge paw prints may be latest evidence of mythical Durham Puma," *Northern Echo* (Priestdale, Darlington, U.K.), July 22, 2009.

2. Paul Sieveking, "Beasts in Our Midst," *Fortean Times*, no. 80 (April–May, 1995), 37–43.

3. Glenda Cooper, "On the Trail of the Beast of Bodmin Moor," *The Independent* (London), February 23, 1995.

4. ITV (Independent Television) *News*, U.K., April 21, 1994.

5. Jeff Schogol, "What Are Those Big Cats U.S. Troops Are Seeing Around Kandahar?" *Stars and Stripes* (Washington), September 9, 2011.

6. "The Eastern Panther: A Question of Survival," *North American BioFortean Review*, Vol. 3, no. 2, issue 7 (October 2001), 29.

7. Leonard McNeill, "Island Harbour," *Them Days*, Vol. 24, no. 2 (Winter 1999), 13.

8. Mina Hubbard, *A Woman's Way Through Unknown Labrador* (London: John Murray, 1908), 76.

9. Bryan A. Greene, "Toponymy from the Mina Benson Hubbard Expedition to Labrador, 1905," *Regional Language Studies Newfoundland*, no. 19 (September, 2006), 4.

10. Brian Kemp, "Big Cat Tales," *Times Globe* (Saint John), August 26, 1998.

11. Luke Ford, Ufodna.com (*thecid.com/ufo/uf19/uf8/198289.htm*), September 1999.

12. Personal communication, August 2000.

13. Ibid., September 2011.

14. William Clarke, "Big Black Cat Sightings Continue Around Region," *Nor'Wester* (Springdale, NL), October 22, 2008.

15. Ibid.

16. Ibid.

17. *Backtalk*, VOCM Radio (St. John's, NL), June 19, 2008.

18. Clarke, "Big Black Cat Sightings Continue Around Region."

19. *VOCM News*, VOCM Radio (St. John's, NL), October 1, 2008.

20. William Clarke, "Big Cat Concerns Prompt Official Reaction." *Nor'wester* (Springdale, NL), November 6, 2008.

21. Ibid.

22. Ibid.

23. "Basic strategy," *The Telegram* (St. John's, NL), November 8, 2008, A27.

24. William Clarke, "Mystery Cat in Springdale Not a Nice Kitty: Resident," *The Western Star* (Corner Brook, NL), December 3, 2008.

25. Aaron Beswick, "People Report Large Black Cat Sightings on Peninsula," *Northern Pen* (St. Anthony, NL), January 26, 2009.

26. Ibid.

27. Ibid.

28. Ibid.

29. Anonymous, personal communication, 2010.

30. Response to "People Report Large Black Cat Sightings on Peninsula," *The Western Star*, October 8, 2011.

31. Ibid.

32. Ibid.

chapter

seven

ODDITIES AND ENT*i*TIES

REPORTS OF STRANGE BEASTS have been numerous throughout our history, and some of these have been placed in various
categories, rightly or wrongly, but this final chapter is a catch-
all. Stories, some of which may not bear the cryptozoological
stamp but are too interesting to ignore and did not fit into the
previous chapters, are included here. Among these strange or
anomalous tales are some that may have a sound basis in fact;
thus, many myths may not be myths at all.

An extraordinary legend of an "elephant monster" exists
among the Innu. Where and how would the Innu encounter an
elephant? Better yet, how would they have recognized it as an
elephant if they did see one? It seems that their description
closely fitted that of a wooly mammoth, and accordingly, was
translated into English as "elephant."

Many Innu and Inuit legends detail nightmarish acts on
the parts of both man and beast; this one concerns a man and
wife who went in search of wood to make snowshoe frames,
leaving their daughter at home. It was their bad luck that an
elephant heard the pair cutting trees, found them, and in a most

The splendid woolly mammoth at the Royal British Columbia Museum, Victoria. Could this be the Elephant Monster of Innu legend?

unelephant-like fashion killed and ate them. While devouring the woman, who was pregnant, the rogue pachyderm came upon her womb, ripped it out, and tossed it into a snowbank. When her parents did not return, the girl, certain they had been caught and eaten by the elephant, wondered what had become of the baby her mother had been carrying. At once, she set out to search and eventually found the child and took him home. The discarded baby matured quickly and grew up to be the Innu folk hero Tshakapesh, who set out on a gruesome career of his own and eventually slaughtered the Elephant Monster.[1]

Many of these extraordinary tales have been passed down for millennia, and as unlikely as it might seem, they may well have been based on fact. Until recently it had been generally accepted that the woolly mammoth (*Mammuthus primigenius*) disappeared from Europe and Southern Siberia about 10,000 bce or at the end of the ice age. They were also supposed to have gone from continental Northern Siberia and North America by that same time, but newfound evidence indicates that some were still present there as late as 8,000 bce.

Yet recently, scientists were floored when they discovered that a small population of woolly mammoths had survived on St. Paul Island, Alaska, until 3,750 bce, while another group lingered on Russia's Wrangel Island until as late 1,750 bce. Can it be there was a Labrador woolly mammoth contemporary with the ancestors of today's inhabitants, and which inspired this legend? Is it reasonable to suppose the story, edited somewhat through tellings, is based on fact?

The mammoth was not our only representative of what we might term "megafauna." Until around ten thousand years ago, a giant beaver (*Castoroides obionensis*) ranged from the Yukon, south to Florida, and from New York west to Nebraska. The size of a black bear, it was more than two metres long and may have tipped the scales at more than 300 kilograms. Its cutting teeth were 15 centimetres long, and its tail was round rather than flat.[2] To judge by recent fossil discoveries, it survived right up until the last ice age, when it disappeared along with the woolly mammoth, giant sloths, and other over-sized mammals. Some authorities believe they died off, not only because the herbage they fed upon became buried beneath glaciers, but because they were hunted to extinction by hungry humans. Scrutiny of legends (once common among northeastern Algonquian tribes, the Innu, and the Mi'kmaq) and a study of the nature and distribution of this Pleistocene colossus have led to the conjecture that elements of these tales represent a kind of fossil memory of such an animal.

However, reports of these huge rodents persisted until the 19th century.[3] In the folklore of the Innu exists the tale of a shaman who dwelt near the mouth of the river at the west end of Shipiskan Lake, some 40 kilometres northeast of the corner of what is now the Smallwood Reservoir. Giant beaver in the area were said to be causing much damage with their enormous dams and phenomenal need for sustenance. The shaman, the only mortal who could kill these walking appetites, managed on one occasion to bag two of them. Of course the natives, provident as they were at that time, ate them. The Innu contend that had the shaman not eliminated that pair there would be a multitude of these creatures lumbering (no pun intended) about today. In any event, from then onward that watercourse became known as Mishtamishku-shipu, or Giant Beaver River.[4]

A variant of the story had Glooskap attempting to kill the beaver but succeeding only in driving them farther west.[5] No matter, it seems they have now vanished and we must be content with the entirely innocuous *Castor canadensis*, our ordinary old nickel-embellishing beaver.

It is possible another strange creature from native mythology has been recorded in our province. *Amarok* is a colossal wolf in the mythology of the Inuit. Moravian missionary Jens Haven, who arrived in Labrador in 1764 and remained to work among the Inuit for the next 20 years, wrote of the *Amarok*:

> All the quadrupeds of Greenland which I could enumerate to the natives exist in Labrador, and in greater numbers. I saw black bear and wolf skins; but the greatest curiosity was the hide of an animal which haunts the Greenlanders in their dreams. They have the same name for it, *Amarok*, and they tremble while they describe it.[6]

Greenland missionary and author David Crantz wrote that this beast was dark grey and about the size of a large dog, but this does not meet the fabulous expectations of the Inuit. Said to prey on and devour anyone imprudent enough to hunt alone at night, it is a solitary and nocturnal killer, unlike the common wolf.[7]

The *Amarok* is considered by some to be the equivalent of *Waheela*, a wolf-like cryptid reported from Nunavut and the Nahanni Valley region of the Northwest Territories. Cryptozoologist Ivan Sanderson thought the latter might represent a relict population of *Amphicyonids*, prehistoric bear-dogs that weighed as much as 200 kilograms. However, these giant wolf-like carnivores of the past have almost certainly been extinct for nearly two million years.

A comparison of the sizes of a giant beaver and a black bear.

A better match would have been the extinct *hyaenodon* (an ancestor of today's hyaena), which were massive brutes and had to be, considering their rivals, the dire wolves and the so-called bear dogs, and their huge prey of woolly rhinoceroses and mammoths. *Hyaenodon gigas*, the largest of the family, was the size of a big bull, and given its heavy coat, which had helped it through the most recent ice age, could easily tolerate the Arctic conditions of the past ten thousand years.

Notwithstanding these possibilities, the most likely candidate for the *Amarok* is the dire wolf, a North American species, which at 85 kilograms was still a great deal larger than today's wolves. For nearly one hundred thousand years, these canids coexisted with their cousins the grey wolves. They are thought to have died out less than 10,000 years ago, raising the distinct possibility that it was coeval with the origin of the *Amarok* legends.

In fact, not long ago, the skeletal remains of a large canid, finally identified as those of a dire wolf, were found in a cave in West Virginia. However, radiocarbon-dating the bones indicated the animal had been alive in the mid-17th to the early 18th century. Europeans had not yet penetrated beyond the Blue Ridge country when the wolf died, but it had certainly been contemporary with humans.

We know for a fact that through the 18th and 19th centuries wolves were rare in Newfoundland; by 1930 they had disappeared entirely, at least according to the experts of the day. That being so, Roland Reid of Bide Arm, out searching for worthwhile timber near Roddickton in 1950, got a bit of a shock on his return trek. A storm had sprung up, and while he was wading through 25 centimetres of snow, he saw a big doglike animal creeping toward him. It was of a sort he had never seen before and it took some time before it dawned on him that it was not a dog at all but probably a wolf; a very large wolf.

These handsome fellows, dire wolves, were the largest true wolves to have lived.

The long-extinct Newfoundland wolf.

Preparing to defend himself with his axe, he glanced to one side and saw two more, even bigger, gliding silently through the trees. When the first leapt at him from only a couple of metres away, he shouted and swung his axe. The beast avoided the blow and fell over a snowbank; the others followed it as it ran off.

Reid, thinking they would make another attempt to get him, called out to his brother, who was not far away loading their sled with wood. His shouts went unheard, and the three animals quickly regrouped to follow him, off to one side, for some time as he continued through the woods.

When he reached his brother, he told him what had happened. They immediately went back to look for the supposed wolves, but there were only paw prints to be seen. Returning to the logging camp, they told the story to the rest of the crew; two men with rifles went out to investigate, but they found nothing. Still, tracks of the beasts were seen in the area for months, and dogs seemed to fear the track-makers, but they were never identified or seen again.[8]

As we suspect in the case of *Amarok*, many a legend has proven not to be a legend at all. For years Labrador natives told of a dreadful, great brown bear living there, and for years men of science declared that such a thing did not exist. Despite the accounts of various Hudson's Bay Company men, many Moravian missionaries, and Captain George Cartwright himself (who described it as a very ferocious bear with a white ring around its neck), authorities remained skeptical.

John Maclean (1799–1890) of the Hudson's Bay Company, having attained more knowledge than the experts during his years in the north, wrote: "The black bear shuns the presence of man and is by no means a dangerous animal; the grisly [sic] bear, on the contrary, commands considerable respect from the 'lord of creation'...."[9]

Apparently, it once haunted the barrens inland from Nachvak, and the natives, whose legends are often unexpectedly accurate, said it was larger than a polar bear (*Ursus maritimus*), much stronger, and would attack men on sight, which polar bears seldom do.

But legends are legends, and no one took the time to investigate nor was there a pressing need to do so. The Ungava barren-ground grizzlies (*Ursus arctos*) were identified by another Hudson's Bay Company factor as early as the 1840s, and natives easily perceived the difference between the ferocious brown bears of the open country and the more timid black bears of the forest. Probably these bears were never numerous, for early naturalists passed along accounts garnered from the natives rather than tales of their own encounters with the big bruins. By the 1920s, the barren-ground grizzlies were gone from the lands east of Hudson Bay, and most doubted that they had ever existed.

Then, in the summer of 1975, the well-preserved skull of a small grizzly bear was found by archaeologist Steven Cox while he was excavating an 18th-century Eskimo midden at Okak Bay. The skull represented the first concrete evidence that the species had once existed east of Hudson Bay during the Holocene period, and it confirmed the long-standing rumours that a Labrador-Ungava barren-ground brown bear did exist, or at least it had existed, and recently too.

So these bears really did prowl Labrador. Dr. Alasdair Veitch, who studied bears of the region in 1989, suspected they were probably victims of over-hunting. The early 20th century saw a steep decline in caribou herds in the vicinity, and this loss of their most important food source certainly did not help preserve the breed.[10]

From fossil evidence, we know that a great variety of truly large animals once existed; no corner of the globe lacks examples. Many of these giants lived during the last ice age – some of them ten times the size of their surviving relatives with which we are familiar,[11] but some of them may have been much smaller.

Anthropologist William D. Strong, of the Field Museum of Natural History in Chicago, accompanied the Rawson-MacMillan Expedition on the schooner *Bowdoin* in 1927–28. He reported that dwarf caribou were seen on occasion and were sometimes killed. Tracks, mixed with those of normal caribou, were their exact duplicates but for size.

For a while it was suspected these creatures might be survivors of Grenfell's grand reindeer experiment of 1908; however, the theory was set to rest to some degree by members of the Innu Traditional Knowledge Committee who took part in the environmental impact study for the Lower Churchill project in 2008.

They spoke of the dwarf caribou, as they did the *matau-uapush* (dwarf rabbit) and *matau-kaku* (dwarf porcupine). The Innu claim these *matau-atiku* are borne by the *napeu-atiku*, or caribou stag, for six years in a sac in their skin; when the stag dies, the matau-atiku emerges from the animal. The newborn is an exact replica of an adult caribou, complete with antlers, but is about the size of a small dog. Evidently, these *matau-atiku* are usually seen amid large herds of everyday caribou, and these latter appear to be their protectors. The skins of these creatures never have holes caused by the bott fly since, apparently, they are somehow impervious to the assaults of that pest.[12]

The infamous grizzly bear.

Mother and father of the matau-atiku?

One man presented what he considered to be further and concrete evidence of such a creature by stating, "My grandfather Shimun killed a big stag. It had a lump on the side that contained a ball of caribou hair. That might have been part of the dwarf caribou."[13] Knowledge of the dwarf caribou and these other animals has been recorded throughout Innu territory. Daniel Clément has also documented the same traditional knowledge among Innu on the Quebec North Shore in his study of 1991.[14]

More bizarre is the lake known as *Atamipekutiku katat*, "where the underwater caribou lived," 150 kilometres north-north-west of Happy Valley-Goose Bay. Here, an Innu saw what he termed *atamipekutiku*, or "underwater caribou," whose

186

tracks in the sand along the shore led into the water but did not emerge. He assumed the caribou lived like a fish, and elders agreed, hence the odd toponym.

As we have seen, the uncommon can sometimes be frightening. Witness the story of a white salamander (*utshishkatataku*) found up the Kenamu River (*Tshenuamiu-shipu*). Several past events concerning these amphibians were also commented upon by members of the Traditional Knowledge Committee:

"Have you heard a story from our grandfathers of a *utshishkatataku* on *Tshenuamiu-shipu*? They say it is small like an otter...I heard she got bitten by it when she was removing the boughs from an old camp site."

Another individual said that he, too, had seen something there, and he gave an unusual description of the presumed amphibian: It was "about the size of a baking powder can," but it was long, slender, and white. When they failed to kill it with a salmon spear, they cut it in half, but to their amazement the pieces came together again of their own volition resulting in an intact – in fact, a completely uninjured – utshishkatataku. Finally, and ironically, in defiance of the Indo-European legend of the salamander springing from fire, someone threw gasoline on it and set it ablaze, destroying the unusual amphibian.[15]

Some think it was possibly a blue-spotted salamander (*Ambystoma laterale*) or a variation, which, though rare, is native to those parts of Labrador. However, one would think that the Innu would be familiar enough with other inhabitants of their land to recognize it.

Not only is our land host to extraordinary life, but our surrounding water also has its share of the more uncommon creatures – many, as discussed above, considered monsters. Perhaps surprisingly, at times some of the ordinary are found to be more diverse in design than we ever suspected.

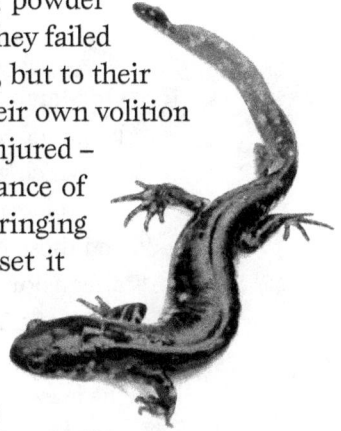

One category of sea creature identified by Bernard Heuvel-mans has four flippers, a tortoise-like head, large prominent eyes, wide mouth, no teeth, and produces a whistling sound as it breathes through its mouth. With a relatively slender, medium-length neck and a rounded carapace with a sawtooth ridge, it certainly fits the description of a turtle. But such a turtle! According to George Eberhart, Columbus saw one in September 1494, off the coast of the Dominican Republic. It was whale sized and kept its head out of the water. It had a long tail with a fin on either side.[16]

In 1883, and much closer to home, the schooner *Annie L. Hall*, Captain Augustus Hall, out of Gloucester, sighted what appeared to be a capsized vessel on the Grand Banks. Upon investigation, however, it was found to be a "trunk turtle," that is, a leatherback (*Dermochelys coriacea*).[17] *Scientific American* and *The New York Times* carried a report of Captain Hall's discovery about a month later. The latter had this to say:

> On March 30, while on the Grand Bank in latitude 40° 10', longitude 33°, they discovered an immense live trunk turtle, which was at first thought to be a vessel bottom up. The schooner passed within 25 feet [8 metres] of the monster, and those on-board had ample opportunity to estimate its dimension by a comparison with the length of the schooner. The turtle was at least 40 feet [12 metres] long, 30 feet [9 metres] wide, and 30 feet [9 metres] from the apex of the back to the bottom of the under shell. The flippers were 20 feet [6 metres] long. It was not deemed advisable to attempt its capture.[18]

Here, as in other sources, the coordinates quoted are some-what awry. These would put the vessel, which was presumably headed for home, some distance to the east-southeast of the Grand Banks. To further complicate things, this story became confused in contemporary newspapers with a more conventional 30-metre-long sea monster seen by Captain W. L. Green and some fishermen off the coast of New Jersey in November of that year.

The giant turtle was nearly forgotten for three-quarters of a century, but in June 1956, interest was suddenly reawakened. The Liberian-registered freighter SS *Rhapsody* reported a 14-metre-long turtle with a white carapace just south of Nova Scotia. Its flippers were said to be four-and-a-half metres long and it raised its head about two-and-a-half metres above the surface.[19] After seeing this report, Dr. Shuker wrote about a witness from the third century, a man named Aelian, who told of huge turtles more than seven metres long swimming about the Indian Ocean. Another story from the same area, by one el Edrisi of Sri Lanka in 1154, had female turtles that were more than nine metres long navigating those waters.[20]

The trunk or leatherback turtle.

The rare beaked whale.

In the late Mesozoic, the largest known turtle, *Archelon ischyres*, was about five metres long, four metres wide, and may have weighed five tonnes. That was some 70 million years ago, and in a reverse twist on the usual giants of the past, modern day reports indicate that sea turtles may reach much larger dimensions now than in prehistoric times. If such creatures exist today, having survived for unknown millions of years, they may be on the way out at last. Leatherbacks are an endangered species, and many die each year by ingesting floating plastic bags which they mistake for jellyfish, their usual diet.

Another intriguing case is that of a little-known whale that showed up off our coasts and then vanished. A gam of what has been called the white-flippered beaked whale – about ten metres long, black above and white below, with white flippers and a long pink-tipped snout – followed an English vessel on a voyage to Jamaica in the 1840s. Naturalist and science populariser Philip Henry Gosse was on board and had the good luck of studying them for a surprising 17 hours.

Tentatively identified as a whale and not suspected of being a mysterious sea monster, it has probably been seen by others since, but if so, no documentation has been found.[21] The report from this single sighting of one of our larger mammals provides the sum total of our knowledge of it.

A different whale story came to the world's attention in 1947. The June issue of *Natural History* magazine carried a letter from a Dr. Davis, who told of an occurrence much more than on the far side of rarity. Apparently, a sperm whale – certainly a monster of sorts – overstepped the bounds of whale-dom and swallowed a man.[22]

The letter was in response to a similar tale, published in an earlier issue of the magazine, and which had caused some discussion as to its veracity. In his letter, Davis stated that in late winter of 1893 or 1894, he had sailed from St. John's on the

The whale fishery.

Newfoundland sealing schooner *Toulinguet* as surgeon, as much for the adventure as for a share of the profits. On the voyage, he had witnessed the demise of a man from Argentia, a sealer on another ship, who fell from a pan of ice into the water near a sperm whale. The whale, confused and irritated by being lost amid the chaos of the seal hunt, bolted the sealer down without hesitation, but was then shot by the swivel-gunner of another ship. The mortally wounded animal swam five kilometres out to sea and was found the following day by men in a longboat. The huge creature could not be dragged back to the schooner, but they did manage to hack their way into its stomach and recover the man's body. Davis examined the corpse (here followed a lengthy and macabre description of what a body might look like having emerged from such a prison) and because of its condition the man was buried at sea. The letter was signed Egerton Y. Davis, Jr., Boston, Mass.

A letter in a later edition of *Natural History* pointed out that the name "Egerton Y. Davis, Jr.," was certainly spurious. Without the "Jr.," it was a *nom de plume* used by famous Canadian surgeon Sir William Osler to lend credence to some of his wild yarns. But Osler had been dead since 1919, so the use of that specific name was an unwise choice if the writer expected his yarn to be taken seriously.

This was a particularly well-told story as, subsequently, it was repeated by the normally cautious Paul Budker in his book, *Whales and Whaling*, and a more famous source seemed to back it up: Jacques Cousteau dealt with the same event in his book, *Whales*.

It is impossible to *disprove* such tales, and they are sometimes even used to *prove* the Biblical story of Jonah and the whale. Nearly all parts of the yarn are plausible, but no record can be found of the schooner *Toulinguet*, of this incident, or even of Dr. Davis. While sperm whales are known to have swallowed giant squid, these are slippery, squishy, and mostly arms and tentacles, while men wear rough clothing and are solid and lumpy. Despite the seemingly authenticated stories (and there are many) no *bona fide* instance of a man being swallowed by any cetacean has come to light. There is, of course, the very remote possibility than an unknown animal, other than a whale, achieved this feat.

Quite recently scientists were at a loss to explain what appeared to be the skeleton of a large mammal protruding from an iceberg that drifted past Newtown on the island's northeast coast. On May 27, 2007, Donna and Eli Norris were in a small aluminum boat, and being both experienced and cautious, they did not want to get too near the berg, though the object was foreign to them. However, Donna took six pictures of what looked like a rib cage and spinal column, the exposed portion of which stuck out of the ice about two-and-a-half metres with the lower part hanging in the water.

Strange skeleton seen by Donna and Eli Norris.

Ruth Knee, a friend of the Norrises, sent the photos to the provincial Department of Fisheries and Aquaculture for identification, but its experts could reach no consensus. Dr. Garry Stenson, of the federal Department of Fisheries and Oceans, said he had not previously encountered a creature of this sort. According to *The Telegram* of June 4:

> Marine scientists in Canada and abroad are puzzled by bizarre photographs that appear to show the skeleton of a large mammal jutting out of an iceberg that recently drifted past Newfoundland's east coast...But researchers throughout Canada, Greenland and Norway are unable to determine the origin of the skeleton, said Garry Stenson, a marine mammal scientist with the federal Fisheries Department.[23]

Some thought it might be the remains of a walrus or a bearded seal, but Stenson disagreed, as did other authorities. It also did not appear to have the bone structure of a whale. Those involved agreed on only three things: They were uncertain as to what the creature was, how long it had been there, or how it came to be frozen into the 10,000-year-old ice. The unconcerned iceberg continued on its journey and was not seen again.

Another unusual mammal, the horsehead seal or grey seal (*Halichoerus grypus*), was recorded in Newfoundland waters at least as early as the mid-1800s. In fact, it was said to have been somewhat common along the east coast. Canon George Earle said that Bill Donahue of Little Fogo Island saw one of these rare creatures, "as long as a punt" and with a mane like that of a horse. He was afraid to shoot at it as he believed that, if he failed to kill it, it would probably turn on him. Earle thought this curious creature might explain some stories of the sea monster variety.[24]

This seal was discussed in the July 1929 issue of *National Geographic*, and in 1960 *The Evening Telegram* described it in detail:

The alien of all the seal species is the horsehead. Many people in Newfoundland have never seen or heard tell of one. I have seen only one such seal in many years of the seal hunt. In fact, I could not name it until an old Port aux Basques seal hunter named it for me...It has a long head exactly like a horse, and the nails on its flippers are more than twice as big as those of a harp seal. The hair on its body is more than twice as long as that of a harp or hood. They pup about the middle of February, and have never been known or seen in large numbers.[25]

This big seal is wary of humans. It can reach as much as three metres in length and weigh up to 420 kilograms; while they are not small animals, they are not of the proportions generally credited to sea monsters.

At times, other odd seals have shown up. On April 16, 1876, a seal with but one eye was brought in by Captain S. Walsh of the SS *Merlin*. More unusual than it having one eye was the fact that it was in the middle of the animal's forehead – a true cyclops.[26]

Under the heading of "Unusual seals," the following appeared in the *Twillingate Sun* of May 31, 1884:

Two remarkable freaks of nature could have been seen on board the S.S. *Falcon* this morning. One was a Siamese twin seal, having two heads, four eyes, eight flippers, two tails; and being eighteen inches in length. It was taken from one of the *Ranger*'s pans, having been killed by one of the latter's crew. Another seal had two flippers on its back, but possessed no tail. Both have been preserved.[27]

While hardly in the class of sea serpents, a very large young hood seal that turned up at New Bay in the spring of 1888 may have been the cause of some strange reports. A young man brought in a seal with, again, eight flippers, two heads, and hind knuckles as large as those of an old seal. On each knuckle were two flippers, and it had two fore-flippers on each side as well. Dead when discovered, it had been partially eaten by crows[28] (such seals would have been a blessing in the flipper market). All this took place long before the spectres of chemical pollution and radioactive spills from nuclear reactors began haunting us.

Seals are not the only cyclopean creatures around our island. In the 1930s, many men from nearby communities worked at the St. John's waterfront. Richard Westcott told of longshoremen from Petty Harbour who walked the 15 or so kilometres home each Saturday evening after work, then returned on Sunday evening. One of these men, a friend of his father, told him of a disturbing experience he had along the road.

Though lame, he walked with the others, but for one Saturday when he was late and they had gone on without him. He made his way along Kilbride Road, up Kenna's Hill, and around the turn to Long Pond where he stopped at the Little Well for a drink of water. As he was about to kneel, he saw a huge creature across the road that was taller than any horse he had ever seen and it had a single eye, the size of a saucer, which was staring straight at him.

Fear of death focuses the mind wonderfully: So terrified was the longshoreman that he forgot he was lame, and ran, tripping over bushes and stones, until he reached Petty Harbour. Gaining the safety of home, he wrenched the door open and fell inside. His concerned father helped him to his bed where he was confined for two months recovering from the mental and physical stress brought on by this alarming experience.[29]

Sometimes non-mythical creatures cause great consternation, too. Around 1850, the road from Broad Cove (today's St. Philip's) to St. John's was haunted by a birdlike monster that attacked pedestrians and horse-cart drivers on dark nights. For several months the "devil on wings" clawed and bit its way to infamy. Many badly frightened travellers became hesitant to take the road by night or by day.

Sadly, it never quite made it into the menagerie of the

strange and unexplained fauna of our province. The mystery was solved when a man took shelter in the trees from a sudden storm and was set upon by the creature. Having lost his whip, in desperation he threw a fishnet over his attacker, entangling it, and then bound it with twine.

In St. John's, he displayed his torn coat and scratched hands, arms, and face, and led his friends to his cart where he showed them the devil. It took a half-dozen men to free it from the mesh, while avoiding the vicious-looking talons and beak. His catch was a

The black vulture can be a fearsome adversary.

huge black vulture (*Coragyps atratus*) with a wingspread of around two metres. While it produced the usual irrational and superstitious yarns, it had doubtless been blown off course and was acting in what it perceived to be self-defence. Released, the bewildered creature flew off not to be seen again.[30]

Other foreign and airborne creatures showed up on August 30, 1855, when swarms of an unidentified insect devastated crops and even filled houses in the settlements of the southern Avalon Peninsula. Dismayed residents tried in vain to clear them from their homes but were generally unsuccessful. The insects left when they were good and ready. Where the bugs came from, what they were, and the full extent of their damage was not recorded.[31]

Small beasties, reminiscent of the Yukon's ice worms, put in an appearance between Portugal Cove and Torbay on February 16, 1888. Hordes of unfamiliar grubs were found on the snow, but again, no one thought to preserve one for potential identification. The species and the impetus for their arrival remain a mystery to this day.[32]

Those living in central Newfoundland in the early to mid-1950s were sometimes plagued by deluges of big, winged, black ants (or emmets), many of which were easily two centimetres long. They fell like rain, pelting down upon the delighted residents of duck pens and upon the equally unhappy human occupants of the towns.

Newspapers published nothing regarding the emmets or carpenter ants (*Camponotus*), for such they appear to have been, and they were considered a natural phenomenon. Though common in Eastern Canada and the United States, their numbers and size were far out of proportion to that which might be expected from a local population. At times, they very nearly formed drifts.

Since there appears to be no record of them whatsoever, here is a puzzle of the most mysterious kind. If the creatures had not originated in Newfoundland, where had they come from? The prolific but secret breeding grounds of king-sized ants across the Cabot Strait? In any event, they have not appeared in such numbers since that time.

Something odd cropped up in Lake Melville not so very long ago. While not mythical or even a true monster, it was disconcerting to Albert "Roy" Powell of North West River. Over the 2010 Easter weekend, Powell took himself a kilometre or so out on the salt water lake with the idea of catching a few tom cod. It was a fine day, the fish were biting, and catch a few tom cod he did, but while cleaning one he was startled to find what appeared to be a sort of bug, nearly eight centimetres long, in its stomach. He had never seen anything like it before. From its head to its tail it was covered with seven rows of scales, had seven legs arranged along each side, and a jointed tail protruding from beneath the rearmost scales. Its mouth appeared to be that of a scavenger or filter feeder.

He took it home and showed it to friends and neighbours, and all were baffled. Lewis Brown of Happy Valley, in his

A trilobite of the sort found in Labrador.

eighties and familiar with most everything that swam, crawled, or flew in Labrador, admitted that he was stumped.

A call was placed to the Department of Fisheries and Oceans, and upon hearing a description of the beast, someone identified it as a trilobite, meaning a creature having "three lobes." They constitute a well-known fossil group of marine arthropods that form the class *Trilobita*. Dr. Robert Hooper, director of Memorial University's Bonne Bay Marine Station, examined the photographs and confirmed that Powell had captured one of these crustaceans, in this case a member of the isopod family. Most residents of this province are familiar with a more common variety of this creature, the woodlouse or carpenter (*Isopoda*).

Powell, like many others, believed that these primitive animals – whose fossilized form is often found – were extinct. However, some have proven to be very obstinate survivors, among them his find and another, a distant cousin, the horse-shoe crab.

Hooper said the bug was unusual mostly because it was armour-plated and about six times larger than the usual isopod, which is commonly over a centimetre long. He also thought that the heavy armour was indicative of a salt-water species, as those living in fresh water would not get the calcium required to produce such scales. He added, "There are a lot of animals on the seabed in Labrador that are really interesting, and there has been very little research...."[33]

Confirmation is hard to come by, but as startling as that critter was, there are creepier things out there. For example, in early April 2010, a remotely operated vehicle exploring the ocean's depths returned with an unexpected passenger that horrified some surface-bound explorers. A technician explained that the creature had attached itself to the ROV at a depth of about 2,600 metres and was inadvertently brought to the surface. It was a little more than three-quarters of a metre long and was identified as *Bathynomus giganteus*, a deep-sea scavenger of a similar type.

A vaguely worded Internet posting sparked concerns that the photos may have been an April Fools hoax. However, Craig McClain, Assistant Director of Science for the National Evolutionary Synthesis Center in North Carolina, said, "I've seen the pictures, and they are real, and they really do get that big." McClain added, "It's an isopod...like the woodlice that you find in your garden. It's the same group of animals. It's definitely not an April Fools' joke." The species was discovered more than a century ago by Alphonse Milne-Edwards, a French zoologist, and it makes our Lake Melville specimen look pretty puny, but when one does not expect to find such a thing, ours can still be perceived as a monster of sorts.

Not only have we hosted strange animals, but strange people as well. Somewhere in the White Bay area, the Norse met some uncommon beings other than the *skrælings* they had reported. This is attested to by the record of an encounter with a "uniped" or "one-footer" (*Einfoetingr*), and by subsequent reference to the country thereabouts as One-footer Land (*Einfoetingr Land*).

According to the *Saga of Thorfinn Karlsefne*, Thorvald Eiriksson and his people were navigating a river when they spied something moving in the woods and shouted at it. They were thunderstruck when a uniped, armed with a bow, hastened down the riverbank toward them. Thorvald, standing at the helm, had an arrow shot "into his bowels" by the belligerent one-footer and died shortly thereafter.

The uniped raced away to the north, and Karlsefne and some of his men gave chase. Though they glimpsed him sporadically, the last they saw of him was when he ran out into the bay. It then occurred to the Norse that they were going deeper into uniped country, and rather than risk more lives, they left. The uniped was obviously agile, one leg or no. A fragment of verse from the saga tells part of the tale:

The death of Thorvald Eiriksson.

We men pursued, this is the truth,
A One-Footer who came to the shore,
But the strange man fled,
Running swiftly over the hills,
This we tell you Karlsefni.[34]

It is apparent in passages from certain Icelandic works that, at the time, Vinland was thought to be in some way connected to Africa. The *Sciopod*, Latin for "shade foot," was a relatively passive creature first recorded around 77 ce by Pliny. Said to live in the wilds of what is now Ethiopia, they were small, pale, human-like creatures with only one leg and a giant foot. These unusual folk hopped about on their colossal feet, but also used them as sun shades. *Sciopods* spent several hours a day lying on their backs, huge feet in the air, blocking the harsh North African rays. Extremely powerful, they could kill a man with a single jumping kick. Luckily they ate no meat, or even plants, but existed on the aroma of living fruit exclusively. They can be found mentioned in numerous writings over several centuries; references to them taper off sometime in the Middle Ages.

The one-legged African race was well known in Iceland; and one of that country's writers made reference to that species' custom of using their feet as sunshades. While this may have played some part in the Vinland accounts, it has also been suggested that the one-footer may have found its way into the saga as a good excuse for Thorvald's expeditious departure from these dangerous shores.

What was meant by one-footer is a mystery, but it is possible that it did not literally mean "uniped," as some writers have contended. It may have been a special connotation in Norse usage to designate a man with one leg or who had been crippled, or even a figurative expression of mockery of some peculiarity of the natives. For instance, we do not mean it literally when we describe someone as "pig-headed" or "cold-hearted." The Norse did imply, though, that there was a tribe of them, certainly more than one individual.

Curiously, in 1536, Jacques Cartier returned to France from his Canadian explorations with reports, no doubt from Indians who had related tales of many marvels, such as would whet the appetites of adventurers. He told not only of the "Kingdom of Saguenay," a land of gold and gems, but of a country whose inhabitants were "as white as those of France," of others who lived without food, and of a region that was home

A uniped putting his celebrated foot to good use.

to a tribe of people *who had but one leg*.[35] What Cartier may have meant is equally obscure, but the strange puzzle is compelling.

Before we ridicule these tales, consider this. On January 9, 2008, an extremely reliable Flatrock couple took a walk to the top of nearby Red Head. The going was rough along the steep path, particularly since it was icy and snow-covered. Few had even approached the route since the most recent snowfall, and they were surprised to come across footprints that were unusual in the extreme. Apparently, someone with only a left foot had ascended the slippery path without the aid of crutches or even a cane. The tracks went to the top of the hill and returned. The pair offered no explanation but commented that if it were the work of a prankster, it was a dedicated and spry one.[36] Perhaps someone has an explanation, but none has yet been offered.

There was another case of an "extinct" species being resurrected for a short time: the great auk. This bird, the original penguin (*Pinguinus impennis*), was thought by learned men to be extinct since the mid-1800s. The largest and only flightless member of its family (i.e., the guillemot, or murre, and razorbill), it was 65 to 80 centimetres long and weighed from five to eight kilograms. Their great breeding colonies were common on the rocky coasts and offshore islands of the North Atlantic, in Greenland, Iceland, the British Isles, Scandinavia, and Canada. Wintering as far south as Florida and southern Spain, they returned in spring, and each pair laid a single large egg on bare rock, then tended it throughout their seven-week breeding cycle. Communal when breeding and unable to take to the air for safety, they were slaughtered in their thousands by man, principally during that season. Made use of by early explorers for fresh meat and eggs, by fishermen for bait, and in the late 1700s by commercial feather gatherers, their numbers quickly dwindled. Far from being the victims of Newfoundland fisher men and hunters, as many would have us believe, they were eradicated chiefly by seafarers and fortune-hunters from the northern and western European nations.

The largest and best-documented colony, that on Funk Island, had been destroyed by about 1800, and the last known breeding pair and their one egg were taken on June 3, 1844, on Eldey Rock off southwestern Iceland. For more than four decades, scientists bemoaned the loss of an opportunity to study the birds.

There was nothing mythological about the great auk, but there was an exceptional incident long after it had *The luckless great auk.*

"officially" vanished. In 1888, two men from Fogo, father and son, found a large, unfamiliar, and exhausted bird floating in slob ice. They had no difficulty killing it and taking it home; they cooked it and so provided three good meals for the family. They told no one of their good fortune until after their dinners.

Soon, a telegram arrived from Governor Sir Henry Blake inquiring about the bird. It had been reported as a penguin and the message was soon followed by a very clear drawing of the bird.

Fogo's Magistrate James Fitzgerald was astonished to find the tale had reached St. John's before he or his neighbours had heard it. Upon interviewing the bird's captors, Fitzgerald found that only its head, feet, and wings were left, and these corresponded exactly with those of the great auk. Carefully packing the remains, Fitzgerald sent them off to the governor.

There is no doubt that it was a great auk, but where it came from is still a mystery. Had the gourmands preserved the bird and reported it, it would have brought them the very substantial sum of $200 (about $25,000 in today's wages).[37]

Among numerous yarns from various sources, a particularly grotesque tale stands out. It appears that one night in April

1989, Diana Fleming and her husband were driving along River Road (the only River Road in Newfoundland, known explicitly by that name, is the road at Appleton). It was near midnight, and they had the road to themselves, having seen nothing unusual but a dead cat lying on the gravel shoulder.

Shortly after passing the defunct feline, Diana's husband glanced in the rear-view mirror and caught a glimpse of a shadowy something following their car. He realized at once that whatever it was, it was moving very fast. As it closed the distance, they could pick out details they would rather have not seen. Hairy and standing erect, it raced along on immense hind legs, but more disturbing were its luminous red eyes.

After some seconds (which no doubt dragged by like minutes) their pursuer dropped back and was lost in the darkness. Presently, they saw several other dead cats along the road, which led them to assume the creature had dispatched them but had no appetite for its victims.[38] Though the monstrosity has not been seen before or since, there has been some discussion as to what it might have been. One school of thought is that it might have been what, in recent years, has been labelled a *chupacabra*, or "goat sucker," derived from its alleged habit of sucking blood from goats. This creature is a celebrated cryptid said to inhabit parts of Mexico, Latin America, and even the southern United States; first having been reported in Puerto Rico. What it may have been doing in a virtually goatless Newfoundland and Labrador is beyond our ken; since it had sunk to catching cats, it was obviously desperate.

Then there is the snow wasset. Perhaps we should not dwell too long on the snow wasset (*Mustelinopsis subitivorax*) as described tongue-in-cheek by William T. Cox in 1903. Said to be a migratory animal which winters south of Hudson Bay, it spends the summers in Labrador.

The wasset sleeps through most of the warm northern summer, its rudimentary legs enabling it to creep about and remain in the shade until its hair turns green, then it curls up in a bog. At the first snowstorm, it awakens, sheds its legs, and sets out for southern climes, dipping about in the snow with surpassing skill, surprising burrowing grouse, rabbits, and other varmints. It has a voracious appetite, comparable only to that of the wolverine, but since it is four times as big and forty times as active as the latter, it must eat correspondingly more.

The elusive snow wasset.

The only specimen ever examined by white men was an imperfect skin found by a survey party who saw, and later commented upon in their field report on, a peculiar Indian canoe. It had been made from a single wasset hide, greatly stretched. There being no leg holes in the winter pelt, the hide was particularly well-suited for making such craft.[39] What have we learned here? Do not believe *everything* you read.

Yet, think, how many kilometres have you driven along the supposedly moose-infested highways of the province? How many of these great bumbling beasts have you seen on an average drive? How many do you suppose have seen you? Certainly the ever-vigilant big cats, wary and well-developed primates of the forest, and normally invisible ocean-dwellers would be even more difficult to detect.

It is beyond the scope of this work to explain sightings: nonetheless, some hypotheses have been offered up as maybes – at least until something better comes along.

1. Peter Desbarats, *What They Used to Tell About: Indian Legends from Labrador* (Toronto: McClelland & Stewart Ltd., 1969), 55–58.

2. Jane C. Beck, "The Giant Beaver: A Prehistoric Memory?" *Ethnohistory* 19 (Spring 1972), 109–22.

3. Ibid.

4. Ibid.

5. Ibid.

6. David Crantz, *The History of Greenland* (London: Longman, Hurst, Rees, Orme, & Brown, 1820), Appendix, 292.

7. Carol Rose, *Giants, Monsters, and Dragons: An Encyclopedia of Folklore, Legend, and, Myth* (Santa Barbara, CA: ABC-CLIO, 2000), 15.

8. Roland Reid, *A Cry in the Morning* (Roddickton, NL: published by the author, 1979), 9–10.

9. Lionel Leslie, *Wilderness Trails in Three Continents: An Account of Travel, Big Game Hunting and Exploration in India, Burma, China, East Africa and Labrador* (London: Heath Cranton Ltd., 1931), 197.

10. Carla Helfferich, "Labrador's Barren-Ground Black Bears," *Alaska Science Forum* (February 12, 1992), article 1069.

11. George M. Eberhart, *Mysterious Creatures: A Guide to Cryptozoology* (Santa Barbara, CA: ABC-CLIO, 2002), 192.

12. William Duncan Strong, "Notes on Mammals of the Labrador Interior," *Journal of Mammalogy*, 11, no. 1 (February 1930) & William D. Strong, "Deer (Caribou)," *Them Days*, 16, no. 3 (April 1991), 9.

13. Lower Churchill Hydroelectric Generation Project, *Environmental Impact Statement*, Vol. 1, Part B: Project Planning and Description Newfoundland & Labrador Hydro (Ottawa: The Government of Canada & the Government of Newfoundland & Labrador, July 2008), 79.

14. "L'homme-caribou: L'analyse Ethnoscientifique du Mythe," *The Canadian Journal of Native Studies*, 11, no. 1 (1991), 49–93.

15. Lower Churchill Hydroelectric Generation Project, 80.

16. Eberhart, *Mysterious Creatures: A Guide to Cryptozoology*, 170–72.

17. Ibid.

18. "A Monster of the Deep," *The New York Times*, April 27, 1883.

19. Eberhart, *Mysterious Creatures: A Guide to Cryptozoology*, 170–72.

20. Karl P. N. Shuker, *In Search of Prehistoric Survivors: Do Giant 'Extinct' Creatures Still Exist?* (London: Blandford, 1995).

21. Philip H. Gosse, *A Naturalist's Sojourn in Jamaica* (London: Longman, Brown, Green & Longmans, 1851), 3–6.

22. Richard Ellis, *Monsters of the Sea* (Guilford, CT: Lyons Press, 2004), 372.

23. Moira Baird, "Photos Show Skeleton Sticking Out of Iceberg," *The Telegram* (St. John's, NL), June 4, 2007.

24. George H. Earle, *A Collection of Foolishness & Folklore* (St. John's, NL: Harry Cuff Publications, 1988), 56.

25. *The Evening Telegram*, (St. John's, NL), February 29, 1960, 2.

26. Maurice A. Devine & Michael J. O'Mara, *Notable Events in the History of Newfoundland: Six Thousand Dates of Historical and Social Happenings* (St. John's, NL: Devine & Omara, 1900), 77.

27. "Unusual Seals," *The Twillingate Sun*, May 31, 1884.

28. "Oddity," *The Twillingate Sun*, April 28, 1888.

29. Garry Cranford, ed., "Richard Westcott," *Our Lives: Ghost Stories* (St. John's, NL: Seniors' Resource Centre, 2000), 1–4.

30. P. J. Wakeham, *New-Land Magazine*, (St. John's, NL, Spring 1973), 81–83.

31. H. M. Mosdell, *When Was That?* (St. John's, NL: Trade Printers & Publishers, 1923), 97.

32. Devine & O'Mara, *Notable Events in the History of Newfoundland*, 35.

33. Adam Randell, "Creepy Crawler," *The Labradorian*, April 12, 2010.

34. A. M Reeves, N. L. Beamish, & R. B. Anderson, "Saga of Eric the Red," *The Norse Discovery of America* (Stockholm: Norrœna Society, 1906), 228.

35. Hans Holzer, *Ghosts: True Encounters with the World Beyond* (New York: Black Dog & Leventhal Publishers, 1997), 564–65; Reeves, Beamish, & Anderson, "Saga of Eric the Red," 228.

36. Anonymous, personal communication, 2009.

37. "Remarkable Bird – Fogo," *The Twillingate Sun*, March 10, 1888.

38. Jorge Martín, *La Conspiración Chupacabras* (San Juan, Puerto Rico: CEDICOP, 1997).

39. William T. Cox, *Fearsome Creatures of the Lumberwoods: With a Few Desert and Mountain Beasts* (Washington: Judd & Detweiler, Inc., 1910), 39.

VISUAL CREdITS

PAGE 50   Royal Navy files.

PAGE 51   John Bortniak, U.S. National Oceanic and Atmospheric Administration.

PAGE 56   Animal Planet (internet).

PAGE 58   U.S. National Oceanic and Atmospheric Administration.

PAGE 62   Margaret Taylor.

PAGE 65   Margaret Taylor.

PAGE 68   Paul Sherman, Wikispaces.com.

PAGE 74   Athanasius Kircher, *Oedipus Aegypticus* (Rome, 1652).

PAGE 76   Sean Linehan, U.S. National Oceanic and Atmospheric Administration.

PAGE 78   Louis Renard, *Poissons écerevesses & Crabes*, Amsterdam (c. 1754).

PAGE 79   Unknown Russian engraver (c. 1866), New York Public Library.

PAGE 81   John William Waterhouse (1901), Royal Academy of Arts, London.

PAGE 82   Unknown (1700s).

PAGE 83   (top) Ulisse Aldrovandi, *Monstrorum Historia* (1642).

PAGE 83   (bottom) U.S. National Oceanic and Atmospheric Administration.

PAGE 87   Theodor de Bry (1528-1598).

PAGE 90   Phineas T. Barnum, *The Life of P. T. Barnum* (1888).

PAGE 92   Keisuke Ito (1803-1901).

PAGE 94   U.S. National Oceanic and Atmospheric Administration.

PAGE 102   Unknown artist in the style of Olaus Magnus' *Carta Marina* (1539).

PAGE 104   Government of Newfoundland and Labrador.

PAGE 105   Don Esau.

PAGE 107   U.S. National Oceanic and Atmospheric Administration.

PAGE 110   Margaret Taylor.

PAGE 114   U.S. National Oceanic and Atmospheric Administration.

PAGE 120   Ulisse Aldrovandi, *Monstrorum Historia* (1642).

PAGE 121   Le Cire, for Wikipedia Commons (2006) (a repository of free content hosted by Fundación Wikimedia).

PAGE 128   Thomas de Leu, *Grand Insulaire et Pilotage* (1586).

PAGE 129   Drawing by Shanadithit, in James P. Howley, *The Beothucks or Red Indians* (1829).

PAGE 130   Alan Michelin.

PAGE 136 Alfred H. Miles, *Five Hundred Fascinating Animal Stories* (1895), Karen Hatzigeorgiou.

PAGE 138 Royal Canadian Navy files.

PAGE 146 Arminius Young, *A Methodist Missionary in Labrador* (1916).

PAGE 152 Richard Lydekker, *A Hand-Book to the British Mammalia* (1896).

PAGE 154 U.S. Fish and Wildlife Service.

PAGE 156 U.S. Fish and Wildlife Service.

PAGE 157 Greg Goebel from Vectorsite (http://www.vectorsite.net/).

PAGE 161 U.S. Fish and Wildlife Service.

PAGE 162 Gord Lee.

PAGE 170 U.S. Fish and Wildlife Service.

PAGE 176 Wikimedia Commons.

PAGE 178 Omar M. Highley, *Fundamentals of Zoology*.

PAGE 181 Wikimedia Commons.

PAGE 182 Wikimedia Commons.

PAGE 184 Greg Goebel from Vectorsite (http://www.vectorsite.net/).

PAGE 186 public-domain-images.com.

PAGE 187 U.S. National Park Service.

PAGE 189 John Nelson, Earth Connection.

PAGE 190 U.S. National Oceanic and Atmospheric Administration.

PAGE 191 Currier & Ives (c. 1875).

PAGE 193 Eli & Donna Norris.

PAGE 197 public-domain-images.com.

PAGE 199 U.S. National Oceanic and Atmospheric Administration.

PAGE 201 A. M. Reeves, N. L. Beamish, and R. B. Anderson, *The Norse Discovery of America* (1906).

PAGE 203 Ulisse Aldrovandi, *Monstrorum Historia* (1642).

PAGE 205 Canadian Museum of Nature.

PAGE 207 Coert du Bois, *Fearsome Creatures of the Lumberwoods* (1910).

BRUCE HYNES was born in Norris Arm, NL, in 1940. In 1958, he enlisted in the Royal Canadian Corps of Signals at Kingston, and after nine years as a radio operator, he transferred to the Royal Canadian Engineers as a topographical surveyor and photogrammetrist. He retired in 1995, but moved to National Defence Headquarters to work as the editor of a military publication. Hynes is a father of four, and he currently resides in Eastport, NL, with his wife, Margaret.